LOCO REVIEW

2009
edition

Martin Buck

FREIGHTMASTER

PUBLISHING

CONTENTS

Published by :

Freightmaster Publishing
158 Overbrook
SWINDON
SN3 6AY

01793 - 644957

www.freightmasterpublishing.co.uk

First published : December 2008

ISBN : 978-0-9558275-1-8

Printed By :

Stephens & George
Goat Mill Road
Dowlais
MERTHYR TYDFIL
CF48 3TD

Cover Design : Martin Buck
Cover Images : Mark Riley
           Ralf Edge

Note: All dates quoted in the text and
captions relate to 2008, unless
otherwise stated.

PREFACE

Loco Review - 2009 edition, follows on from where the 2008 book leaves off and, as there is so much going on, it has grown in size from 144 pages to a staggering 224 pages - in fact, one contributor likened compilation to *'War and Peace'* and I think he's just about right; I could have taken even more pages, but a halt had to be called at some point!

This pictorial offering, whilst recording the loco-hauled events which help make the rail scene so interesting, enables contributors to showcase their fine imagery and to give readers a taste of the variety of photographic opportunities to be had by the lineside.

Highlights, there are a plenty, too many to list, so here's a snapshot ....

Freight Operations

- Fastline Coal and Class 66/3 locomotives.
- Advenza Freight.
- 2012 London Olympics construction traffic.
- Settle & Carlisle freight flows.

Passenger Operations

- Grand Central HSTs and diesels on the Durham Coast.
- Wrexham, Shropshire & Marylebone Railway top 'n' tail Class 67s.
- National Express franchises.

Plus:

- Plenty of action featuring Class 37s and Class 60s.
- Class 86s & 87s return to main line running.
- Class 40 Golden Jubilee.
- 'Stobart Pulman' charter train.
- Spitfire Railtours diesel-hauled charters.
- Open days, Galas and Heritage Lines

But, don't take my word for it, have a look and judge for yourself.

Work has already started on the 2010 edition, with plenty of interesting action already earmarked for inclusion: Water Cannon, Fastline coal from Avonmouth and Immingham, not to mention ATW loco-hauled passenger services between Holyhead and Cardiff.

With plenty to enjoy, get those cameras primed and ready for action!

Martin Buck

INFRASTRUCTURE & CONSTRUCTION MATERIALS

2012 London Olympics

2012 may well be four years hence, but construction of the Olympic site in the east end of London will gradually gather pace with huge tonnages of raw materials being brought in by rail to complete the project. Many new flows will be introduced to bring in cement (see Page 31), sand, stone and steel.

It is hard to imagine the scale of what is required to get the Olympic Park ready for the Olympic Games. To put the scale of the project into perspective, the infrastructure will be twice that of Heathrow's Terminal 5, but in half the time. It will also be the biggest logistical operation in England since the Second World War.

What makes this project interesting from an enthusiast's perspective is the variety of locomotives and rolling stock, upon which it will be neccesary to call to work these services - many involving wagon types working over routes not normally associated with them, as the images in this section will illustrate to good effect.

Above: *As is so often the case, bad light thwarts the best efforts of the cameraman, who seeks to capture that new working! One such instance is 6Z32, the 11:00 Ripple Lane - Cardiff Tidal steel empties, seen here passing Manor Farm, Cholsey, on 31st July formed of KIA canvas sided steel carriers, hauled by No.47828 'Joe Strummer'. The steel for the Olympic site travels overnight on 6Z31, the 22:15 Cardiff Tidal - Ripple Lane and, during 2008, the train proves to be an irregular runner, to say the least!* **Dave Stracey**

Opposite:

An interesting combination for the 'Berks & Hants' line. Recently outshopped Class 59 No.59005 'Kenneth J. Painter' slowly descends from Savernake Summit towards the site of Wolfhall Junction on 10th October with 7A17, Merehead - Acton formed of two portions of aggregate. The usual 'Yeoman' JHAs are at the rear of the train while the front portion consists of Freightliner HIAs conveying aggregate specifically for use on the London 2012 Olympic project. The train will split at Acton and the HIAs will go forward as 6Z61, the 15:15 Acton - Bow. **Martin Buck**

Previous Page: *The Freightliner HIA bogie hoppers, both the green and the white-liveried examples, are normally associated with the flow of Limestone from Tunstead to power station desulphurisation plants, such as Drax and West Burton, rather than 'off route' as illustrated. On their normal duties, Class 66/5 No.66581 'Sophie' heads westwards though Edale in the Hope Valley on 5th March with 6M96, Drax - Tunstead empty Limestone hoppers; a truly atmospheric shot!* **Fred Kerr**

Above: *One of the first new aggregate flows to start running in conjunction with the London 2012 Olympics is 6Z60, the 10:29 (T/ThO) Bardon Hill - Bow Olympic, which is seen on 4th February with No.60065 'Spirit of Jaguar' passing Sharnbrook on the Midland Main Line, crossing from the 'Up Fast' to the 'Up Slow' line. The train is formed of JNA bogie box wagons.* **Nigel Gibbs**

Below: *On 12th August, there is an unusual sight in the South West of England, Bardon Aggregates JRA bogie hoppers, numbered in the RIV (International standard) system, which are normally seen on the Midland Main Line carrying stone from Croft to Bow. Freightliner's Class 66/6 No.66620 passes Brent Knoll with 6Z60, the 10:25 Bow - Hackney Yard sand empties, formed of these JRA wagons.* **Chris Perkins**

Above: *A truly coulourful scene; hired-in DRS Class 66/4 No.66428 approaches the well known vantage point of Mill Road, Wellingborough, hauling a rake of loaded MJA bogie box wagons on 14th August, running as 6L84, the 08:55 Croft - Bow Olympic. Note the wind turbines punctuating the skyline in the distance.* **Andy Small**

Overleaf: *Another offering from Wolfhall on the 'Berks & Hants', but this time a landscape view. The harvest has been gathered in and there is a hint of Autumn in the air as Class 59/2 No.59206 'Pride of Ferrybridge' hauls an additional 6Z34, the 10:04 (ThO) Merehead - Bow on 27th September.* **Martin Buck**

Below: *Class 66/0 No.66020 heads along the GWML at Spring Farm, Goring, with a rake of MBA 'Monster' box wagons loaded with spoil from the Olympic site on 20th June, running as 6Z30, the 05:03 Bow Olympic - Appleford. One notable service which also uses the Appleford landfill site is the GLC Brentford 'Binliner'.* **Dave Stracey**

EWS MLAs

Above: *Similar in appearance to MCA / MDA / MOA bogie wagons, EWS take delivery of their new low sided ballast MLAs. On 25th May, No.66176 is seen departing from an engineer's possession at Greenhil on 6K23, Greenhill Junction - Millerhill, and a new rake of MLAs in tow.* **Guy Houston**

Carlisle Sand

Above: *On 1st July, EWS operate a trial trainload of sand from Carlisle to Leeds, using ex-National Power JMA and JHA hoppers, running via the Settle & Carlisle (S. & C.). The sand is understood to be coming by road from Tarmac Northern's Cardewmires Quarry, near Dalston, to Carlisle London Road for loading onto rail wagons, destined for Tilcon's sidings in Hunslet, Leeds. On the day of the trial, No.66034 sweeps over Dandry Mire Viaduct into Garsdale with 6Z71, the 09:56 Carlisle London Road - Leeds Hunslet.*

Previous Page: *This train does not seem to run to any regular pattern but, when it does make an appearance, it provides great photographic opportunities. On 23rd August, No.66034 (again!) is greeted by sunshine as it heads off Ribblehead Viaduct, running on this occasion as 6Z71, the 10:27 Carlisle Yard - Leeds Hunslet.* **Neil Harvey**

Diverted Cement

Above: *The line between Lostock Hall and Blackburn receives little photographic attention, although there are some interesting structures along the route, such as the elevated level crossing frame at Bamber Bridge.*

Bamber Bridge Signal Box is a unique, flat roofed, 3-storey building constructed by the Lancashire & Yorkshire Railway, opening in October 1906. It became Bamber Bridge Crossing Frame in November 1972, at which time a six-switch panel replaced the signal box frame. On 11th June, No.66107 passes with the diverted 6S00, Clitheroe - Mossend cement.
Fred Kerr

Willesden 'Spoil'

Above: *A party of school children have just been for a ride behind "Millom" (Hudswell Clarke 0-4-0ST No.1742/1946) at the Buckinghamshire Railway Centre, Quainton Road. After their visit, they watch from the footbridge as No.60079 'Foinaven' powers through the station with 17 JNA wagons in tow, running as 6Z47, Willesden Powerday - Calvert loaded spoil train, at 12:28hrs on a very windy, Wednesday, 12th March.*

Below: *EWS No.66096 arrives at the Calvert trans-shipment facility with 6Z47 from Willesden at 14:07hrs, almost 90 minutes late (due to arrive at 12:40hrs) on the afternoon of Thursday, 28th February. One of the earth-moving trucks is already standing by the unloading grab waiting to go into action.* **Geoff Plumb (2)**

At The Double!

Above: *This is Eastriggs, near Annan, on 12th June, and the Gretna - Annan section of the ex-Glasgow & South Western route which is being doubled. The train in view is being used to consolidate the new track and shows No.66047 leading with No.66061 trailing with a rake of MRA wagons loaded with ballast. The new doubled track section opens in August.* **Donald Cameron**

Tree Clearance

Below: *There are several lines around the country where encroaching vegetation makes it extremely difficult to secure lineside photographs and two lines in the Midlands readily spring to mind: Water Orton - Nuneaton and the Sutton Park line (Ryecroft Junction - Park Lane Junction). Fortunately, Network Rail have started to cut back some of the trees on the Sutton Park line, which is opening up a few locations. On 27th March, No.60076 with No.66144 DIT heads 6D44, 12:27 Bescot - Toton engineers train past Blackroot Pool.* **Chris Perkins**

'Bisons' on the Move

Above: *On Tuesday, 13th May, DRS operate an additional 'one off' dedicated train of 'Bison' concrete floor sections to Aberdeen for use in the Aberdeen Harbour retail development. The train, 4A64, 07:17 Grangemouth - Aberdeen Craiginches, is seen passing Carnoustie hauled by No.66416 and a consist of flats and curtain side containers conveying the floor sections. In previous weeks, the payload had been 'tagged on' to the existing Aberdeen DRS train but, because this was running near capacity, this one-off train was operated.*

Below: *A close up view of 'Bison' concrete sections.*   **Jim Ramsay (2)**

Woking Direct

Above: *Woking starts to receive its stone direct from Merehead, w/c 10th December 2007, previously sourced as a trip off the jumbo trains via Acton since 2005. On 27th March, Class 59/2 No.59201 'Vale of York' heads 6Z48, the 06:54 Merehead - Woking past Ford, on a line that sees no scheduled freight traffic, save for the odd MoD train to Ludgershall and 6M58, Southampton - Bescot cars, so this is a welcome addition.* **Nic Joynson**

Overleaf: *Here we see the return working (6Z49) passing through Basingstoke on 2nd October, where the main interest is not really the train, but No.59001 'Yeoman Endeavour', which has received a fresh coat of paint sporting the corporate colours of Aggregate Industries, who have recently taken over Foster Yeoman.* **Martin Buck**

Aylesbury Upgrade

Above: *EWS No.60100 'Pride of Acton' is in charge of a train of YDA ballast hoppers as track is upgraded to passenger standards at Rabans Lane, north of Aylesbury on 7th December 2007. This is in connection with the building of the new Aylesbury Vale Parkway station on the former Great Central and Metropolitan Joint Line, which is at present 'freight only' between Aylesbury and Calvert.* **Geoff Plumb**

MAIL By RAIL
325 'Drags'

Above: *The evening of 27th December 2007 marks the end of scheduled Class 87 hauled services and their withdrawal from traffic. No.87028 'Lord President' works the diverted 1A04, 16:12 Shieldmuir - Willesden formed of Nos.325015 + 325007, seen waiting time at Darlington for the last time. No.87022 works north the same evening with 1S04, Willesden - Shieldmuir; the two services passing and changing crews at Darlington.* **Carl Gorse**

Previous Page:

First Great Western Class 57/6 No. 57602 'Restormel Castle' rescues 1M44, the 15:32 Shieldmuir - Warrington mail on 8th May. The units developed a fault and No.57602, which was in the process of returning south after being at Brush Barclay in Kilmarnock, is turned back at Oxenholme to rescue the failed train from Shieldmuir. It is running about 3 hours late passing Lamington, south of Carstairs. **Donald Cameron**

Below: *Arguably the most interesting of the post-Christmas 2007 Class 325 'drags', due to WCML engineering disruption, takes place on 3rd January with 'Metronet' No.66722 rostered to work 1F31, Wembley - Warrington mail in place of the usual class 47. On an absolutely freezing cold day with strong winds, the train is seen entering Berkswell station, running a little under an hour late.* **Peter Tandy**

Above: *Class 47/8 No.47805 'Talisman' is hard on the heels of a Cross Country Voyager as it approaches King's Sutton station on Saturday, 29th December 2007, with 1A84, the 10:19 Warrington RMT - Wembley PRDC Royal Mail train, comprising mail units No.325011 & No.325008. The train is running around an hour late, diverted due to engineering work on the WCML.* **Geoff Plumb**

Below: *A superb shot of a Class 87 at work on the WCML, a month before the axe finally falls. No.87028 'Lord President' passes Blisworth at speed on 29th November 2007 hauling mail units No.325001 and No.325002, forming 1M85, Shieldmuir RMT - Willesden PRDC.* **Ian Ball**

ADVENZA FREIGHT

Late 2007 sees the launch of Advenza Freight, part of Cotswold Rail, with the aim of providing niche services to railfreight customers. In particular, intermodal, high speed and precision logistics distribution throughout the UK, along with the movement of rolling stock for maintenance / storage. Advenza start with a small fleet of four locomotives, two of which being 'surplus to requirements' ex-Freightliner Class 57s:

Number	Class	Livery	Year	Previous Operator
47237	47	Advenza Freight Blue	2007	Direct Rail Services
47375	47	Advenza Freight Blue	2007	FM Rail
57005	57	Advenza Freight Blue	2008	Freightliner
57006	57	Advenza Freight Blue	2008	Freightliner

In March, Advenza start operating scrap metal flows from T.J. Thomsons & Son (Stockton on Tees) to Cardiff Tidal with future trials taking place to move scrap metal from Beeston, Handsworth, Hitchin and Tyne Dock. The initial flow is as follows:

6Z72, 10:25 TThO Stockton - Cardiff Tidal
6Z70, 19:25 SX Stockton - Cardiff Tidal

6Z71, 10:45 Cardiff Tidal - Stockton
6Z71, 17:20 TThO Cardiff Tidal - Stockton

Above: *On Monday, 21st January, No.57005 makes the first appearance for the class at Long Marston and then makes a repeat performance the following day. The move is laid on to take TDAs to Bescot and the rake of 15 tanks is seen here in road 2 of the exchange sidings, with Motorail Logistics crew on hand to make sure all goes well. The 'Advenza Freight' headboard is soon attached to the leading end of No.57005 and, as soon as the driver completes his walk along the train to perform a brake test, 6Z98 will leave for Bescot!* **Peter Tandy**

Above: *Training runs take place in March In readiness for the new scrap metal flows. On St. David's Day, Class 47/0 No.47237 + Class 57 No.57006 double-head 6Z90, the 09:04 Gloucester New Yard – Plymouth training run through Totnes with a rake of 13 KEA wagons.* **Robert Sherwood**

Below: *Four days later, Nos.57006 + 57005 are an impressive sight as they cautiously proceed out of the TJT Thomsons scrap metal terminal with loaded KEAs, forming 6Z75, the 18:20 Stockton - Cardiff.* **Carl Gorse**

Above: On 3rd March, a scheduled 6Z45, Gloucester Yard - Long Marston locomotive & stock move fails to materialise because one of the Class 37s due for movement (No.37704) having seized brakes. The same problem still prevails the following day, so the recalcitrant locomotive is finally shunted out of the consist leaving just No.37898 and four JTA wagons to be moved - seen passing Badgeworth hauled by No.47237, 90 minutes late en route to Worcester Yard for a layover and reversal. **Peter Tandy**

Below: Advenza's newly acquired Class 57 No.57005 (minus her nameplates) is pressed into service on 9th February to move long-stored Cargowaggons from Doncaster to Wembley. The train, running as 6Z57, the 09:00hrs ex-Doncaster, makes its way out of Humberstone Road Yard, Leicester, and onto the Midland Mainline. **Andy Small**

FREIGHT FLOWS

Above: *On 15th August, No.57006 accelerates past Melton Mowbray's impressive signalbox with 6Z55, the 07:30 Cardiff Tidal - Hitchin scrap empties. Melton Mowbray is situated on the former Midland Railway cross-country route between Leicester and Peterborough, a line with plenty of mechanical signalling, the 'boxes at Frisby, Ashwell, Oakham and Langham Junction, readily springing to mind.* **Nigel Gibbs**

'Tesco Express' goes daily!

Above: *Another sign of increased retail growth for Tesco is the start of a sixth day (Saturday) DRS operated 'Tesco Express' service between Daventry and Grangemouth, running in both directions; see Page 104 for more details. This illustration, although not the Saturday train in question, features 4M48, the 17:59 Grangemouth - Daventry 'Tesco Express' passing Beattock Summit on 16th April hauled by No.66414; the southbound 'Tesco Express' is a rarely photographed train, hence the inclusion of this image!* **Keith McGovern**

INTERMODAL

Expansion of Channel Tunnel services

In January, EWS launch a new network of European cross-border intermodal rail freight services, operated by Euro Cargo Rail, connecting key European hubs with Britain. The new intermodal services take advantage of the Channel Tunnel "open access" regime and for the first time Euro Cargo Rail will take full accountability for reliable, integrated rail services with improved transit times and a reduction in operating complexity. Services will be rolled out to connect Belgium, Germany, Italy, France, Spain and Switzerland with the key UK economic regions of the Midlands, North West England and Scotland.

Above: *The 'renaissance' of Channel Tunnel intermodal traffic sees the resumption of 4O33, 03:39 (WSO) Trafford Park - Dollands Moor, which is seen passing Old Linslade hauled by Class 92 No.92019 'Wagner' on 29th March, with a mix of Italian GTS and French CNC curtainsiders bound for Piacenza in Italy.* **Nigel Gibbs**

Below: *Meanwhile, on 12th April, in the heart of Kent, Class 66/0 No.66065 heads another new service, 4O70, (SO) Hams Hall - Dollands Moor (Novara), passing Tutt Hill between Charing and Hothfield.* **Nick Slocombe**

FREIGHT FLOWS

Above: *On 11th February, No.66056 snakes out of Swindon Transfer Sidings onto the mainline in readiness to run round and take empty WIA car carriers the short distance to South Marston. The train is 4V41, Dollands Moor - South Marston, which had run direct to Swindon on this occasion. Meanwhile, No.66021 waits in Cocklebury Sidings with a rake of MBAs loaded with scrap metal, forming 6H56 to Port Talbot.* **Martin Buck**

Above: *Looking back to Mostyn and Point of Ayr, No.60039 runs close to the North Wales coast at Ffynnongroew on 31st May working 6F18, the 14:50 (SO) Holyhead RTZ - Warrington Arpley. The train is formed of nine IWA bogie Cargowaggons, ones which have a distinctive curved roof.* **Neil Harvey**

SOUTH MARSTON HONDAs

Hot on the heels of the Newport ADJ - Swindon (6C01) which commenced last September bringing in steel for the production of Mini car panels at the BMW plant, a second automotive related flow commences in November 2007. Honda export cars for the first time by rail, using the Keypoint Railfreight Terminal at South Marston, which is also the first time rail-borne services have used this purpose built, rail connected, terminal since opening for business several years ago.

The flow utilises the unique blue-liveried, 5-unit, WIA enclosed car carriers, which are used around the country to protect high value cars from vandals. The train runs as:

4O79,	MThO	19:39	South Marston	- Dollands Moor
4V14,	WO	04:56	Dollands Moor	- South Marston

'RTZ' RETURNS TO RAIL

It's good to think that road transport does not always win the day. On 9th February, it was thought the last train of aluminium had run from the Anglesey Aluminium Ltd. smelter near Holyhead, via Warrington and the 'Enterprise' system to Austria. This switch to road transport probably results in some extra 100 lorries travelling along the A55 and M6 as a result.

However, the good news, less than a month later the aluminium traffic returns to rail, which is also good news for enthusiasts, as this train will often produce a Class 37 or 60 locomotive.

6D19,	SO	06:40	Warrington Arpley	- Holyhead
6F18,	SO	14:50	Holyhead	- Warrington Arpley

GMC 'BINS' GO GREEN

Freightliner Heavy Haul take over the Greater Manchester Council (GMC) domestic waste trains ('Binliners') from EWS from April, which leaves only the Brentford - Appleford 'Binliner' under EWS jurisdiction. The three diagrams affected are:

6E01, 01:53 Northenden - Roxby		6M05, 09:30 Roxby - Northenden
6E06, 09:33 Bredbury - Roxby		6M06, 17:07 Roxby - Bredbury
6J45, 18:27 Dean Lane - Pendleton		6E07, 19:33 Pendleton - Roxby
6M07, 11:05 Roxby - Pendleton		6J44, 15:49 Pendleton - Dean Lane

Overleaf:

6E06, Bredbury 'Bins'

Page 28: *On 9th May, No.66530 is seen at Heaton Lodge Junction with one of Freightliner's recent gains from EWS, 6E06, the 10:00 Bredbury - Roxby loaded containerised waste. The train is coming off the single line spur which gives eastbound services access from the Diggle route onto the Calder Valley Main Line. The landfill site at Roxby is situated just under four miles (3m 60ch) along a branch leading off the Stainforth - Barnetby main line at Trent Junction, Scunthorpe.*

Page 29: *A Green machine seemingly in perfect harmony with England's green and pleasant land; No.66526 'Driver Steve Dunn - George' passes Saddleworth, working hard as the train climbs towards Diggle before levelling off for the passage through Standedge Tunnel.* **Neil Harvey (2)**

CEMENT

Moorswater

December 2007 sees rail-borne cement traffic resume from Westbury since the ill-fated 'Piggyback' trial to Southampton in 2003. The flow serves Moorswater and whereas the previous regular flow was mainly bagged cement from Earles, this time it is in the form of bulk cement:

6G22, 18:20 MWO Westbury Cement Works - Moorswater
6C66, 16:33 TThO Moorswater - Westbury Cement Works

Clitheroe

Remember the famous Clitheroe - Gunnie cement trains thrashing up the WCML, hauled by a pair of Class 37s? Well, not quite the same, but after several year's absence, 2008 heralds the return of rail-borne cement out of the Castle Cement Works, Horrocksford, Clitheroe.

This time, a thrice-weekly service will see an EWS Class 66/0 locomotive running between Clitheroe and Mossend, via the Settle & Carlisle, using new purpose built JPA bogie cement tank wagons. The new service is as follows:

6S00, 18:40 MO Clitheroe - Mossend
6S00, 17:11 WFO Clitheroe - Mossend

4M00, 05:02 MO Mossend - Clitheroe

West Thurrock

Cement trains start running in June to a purpose built terminal at West Thurrock on the north bank of the River Thames on behalf of Lafarge and Castle Cement, operated by Freightliner and EWS, respectively. Huge tonnages of cement will be needed for the construction of the London Olympic site and so these new services will be a regular sight in the years leading up to 2012.

FHH	6Z86, 22:28 FX	Earles sidings - West Thurrock
	6Z92, 10:49	West Thurrock - Earles
EWS	6L00, 15:17	Ketton - West Thurrock
	6M00, 00:18	West Thurrock - Ketton

Top Left: *It is pleasing to report the return of rail-borne cement leaving Westbury Cement Works for the first time since 2003 which is a welcome addition to railfreight in the South West of England. On 19th February, the returning empty cement tanks from Moorswater to Westbury (6C66) are seen being hauled by Freightliner's No.66951 on the approach to Powderham foot crossing, just under 2 miles east of Starcross.* **Robert Sherwood**

Bottom Left: *On 9th June, No.66621 shunts cement tanks off 6Z86 from Earles Sidings in the new cement terminal at West Thurrock, situated below an elevated section of the HS-1 and close to the Dartford Road Crossing. The train is made up of PCA wagons rather than newer JPA bogie tank wagons.* **Iain Scotchman**

Above: *On 18th July, No.66183 heads across Whalley Viaduct with 6S00, Clitheroe - Mossend loaded cement. This viaduct is situated on the Blackburn to Hellifield main line, four miles west of Clitheroe and known locally as 'Whalley Arches'. It has 48 spans crossing the River Calder and was built between 1846 and 1850 of red brick arch construction and is the longest and largest railway viaduct in Lancashire; built for the Bolton, Blackburn, Clitheroe and West Yorkshire Railway.* **Fred Kerr**

Opposite: *OK, so for some enthusiasts, it may only be a 'shed', but could one ask for more - perfect weather, beautiful scenery and a new freight service traversing the 'Long Drag'! Looking out across windswept moorland and stone-fenced fields towards Pen-y-Ghent dominating the horizon, No.66110 passes Selside Moor on 7th May with 6S00 loaded cement, formed of unbranded JPAs.* **Neil Harvey**

Below: *On 7th July, No.66221 climbs towards Shap Summit at Greenholme with the diverted 6S00, Clitheroe - Mossend cement. Note the additional catenary stanchion, which has been erected to help support the overhead wires during periods of strong winds.* **Keith McGovern**

Above: *EWS Class 66/0, No.66151 powers south through Great Wymondley, Hitchin, on 21st July leading the first Ketton - West Thurrock loaded cement service in connection with the building work involved for the forthcoming Olympics in 2012. The train runs as 6L00, 15:17hrs ex-Ketton on Monday, Wednesday and Thursday with the empties returning on Tuesday, Thursday and Friday. Unusually, the train travels via Hitchin, whereas the majority of other freight services go via the Hertford Loop. The train is running in the region of 65 minutes behind schedule as it passes the camera.* **James Welham**

Below: *Meanwhile, the Freightliner operated service is illustrated here with No.66529 passing Allsop Crossing, Loughborough, on Friday, 1st August, with 6Z92, the 10:49 West Thurrock - Earles Sidings cement empties, comprising a combination of new JPAs and the older PCAs.* **Andy Small**

COAL

Enter Fastline ....

The long-awaited entry of Fastline in the power station coal market takes place week commencing 12th May. The initial services are rather hybrid as only a handful of new Fastline IIA wagons have been delivered and their own Class 66/3 locomotives had yet to arrive in the UK. Therefore, rakes will be formed of 'spare' GBRf HYAs and worked by 'hired-in' DRS Class 66/4 and GBRf Class 66/7 locomotives.

A typical trainplan, actually for week commencing 13th July, is shown in the table on the right.

Previous Page:

Initially, Fastline coal services are unable to run directly out of Daw Mill to Nuneaton, and have to make the relatively short journey to Saltley (run round) before retracing their steps and proceeding to Nuneaton, thence the Midland Mainline. On 1st July, No.66301 passes Whitacre with loaded hoppers (GBRf HYAs and Fastline IIAs) running as 6D03, the 10:28 Daw Mill - Ratcliffe. **Martin Buck**

Set 1

4G80,	03:24	MO	Chaddesden - Daw Mill
4G82,	01:00	MSX	Ratcliffe PS - Daw Mill
6D00,	07:28	SX	Daw Mill - Ratcliffe PS
4G81,	13:30	SX	Ratcliffe PS - Daw Mill
6D01,	19:27	SX	Daw Mill - Ratcliffe PS
4G82,	01:00	SO	Ratcliffe PS - Hatfield Mine
6D00,	07:43	SO	Hatfield Mine - Ratcliffe PS
4G81,	13:30	SO	Ratcliffe PS - Chaddesden

Set 2

4G90,	04:45	SX	Ratcliffe PS - Daw Mill
6D03,	10.28	SX	Daw Mill - Ratcliffe PS
4G89,	17:00	SX	Ratcliffe PS - Daw Mill
6D04,	23:30	SX	Daw Mill - Ratcliffe PS
4G90,	04:44	SO	Ratcliffe PS - Daw Mill
6D03,	10:26	SO	Daw Mill - Ratcliffe PS
4G89,	16:30	SO	Ratcliffe PS - Chaddesden

Set 3

4G95,	08:16	MTO	Ratcliffe PS - Daw Mill
6D06,	15:46	MTO	Daw Mill - Ratcliffe PS
4G95,	08:16	WThFO	Ratcliffe PS - Hatfield Mine
6D06,	15:00	WThFO	Hatfield Mine - Ratcliffe PS
4G96,	21:00	SX	Ratcliffe PS - Daw Mill
6D08,	03:00	MX	Daw Mill - Ratcliffe PS
4G98,	08:15	SO	Ratcliffe PS - Chaddesden

Above: *The latest additions to Fastline Freight's locomotive fleet are five Class 66/3s, which will initially be put to work on the newly acquired contract to convey coal from Daw Mill and Hatfield to Ratcliffe power station. On 18th July, Fastline-liveried No.66304 heads north through Cossington with 6D03, the 10:28 Daw Mill - Ratcliffe loaded coal, formed entirely of new IIA bogies hoppers.* **James Welham**

Bottom Left: *This is Hoggrills End foot crossing, near Whitacre on the Water Orton - Nuneaton main line, and No.66304 is heading east on 21st July with loaded coal hoppers. This is the second coal service to leave Daw Mill this day - 4G95, 08:16 Daw Mill - Ratcliffe.* **Dave Stracey**

Below: *On 16th July, No.66301 passes under the loading bunker at Hatfield Colliery with 4G95, the 08:16hrs ex-Ratcliffe, prior to returning with 6D06, the 15:00hrs loaded train to Ratcliffe power station.* **Nigel Gibbs**

West Coast MEAs

July sees the start of a second train of coal from New Cumnock using MEA box wagons (the first being in August 2007 to Ketton), but this time running to Newport Docks, where the coal will be blended with Russian coal, destined for Aberthaw power station. The new flow runs as follows:

6M08, 10:11 New Cumnock - Warrington

6Z40, 00:55 Warrington - Newport Docks

6Z41, 15:00 Newport Docks - Ayr

Above: *On 4th August, No.66097 passes Brock, seven miles north of Preston on the WCML, with a rake of loaded MEAs on the first leg of the journey to South Wales, running as 6M08, the 10:00 New Cumnock - Warrington Old Junction Yard. Due to the length of journey, it is intended that this new flow will be able to utilise a second rake of MEAs, so the train can run daily.* **Nic Joynson**

GBRf expansion

Following GBRf's successful move into the coal market in 2007 with their Tyne Dock - Drax services, further new flows commence in 2008. The initial trains are as follows:

6C10, 03:10 SX   Immingham - Eggborough

4N13, 15:08 SX   Eggborough - Immingham

6H20, 07:50 SX   Redcar - Drax

4N20, 15:08 SX   Drax - Redcar

6H21, 20:29 WThFO Redcar - Drax

4N21, 01:50 ThFSO Drax - Redcar

6N98, 10.30 WThFO Widdrington to Lynemouth

4N98, 16.14 WThO Lynemouth to Widdrington

Above: *Metronet-liveried No.66718 'Gwyneth Dunwoody' joins the Knottingley - Goole main line at Whitley Bridge Junction on 22nd April with a rake of HYA coal empties, running on this occasion as 4Z11, Eggborough - Immingham* **Guy Houston**

Below: *Meanwhile, early morning and on the branch, No.66711 approaches High Eggborough with 6C10, the 03:10 Immingham - Eggborough loaded coal train.* **Ian Ball**

Above: *History in the making .... the first coal train travels to Longannet power station by way of the new Stirling - Alloa - Kincardine line on 5th April. The normal 7G18, 13:00 departure from Hunterston is recoded to 6G18 and a consist of 21 HTAs instead of the normal 39 HAAs. Here it is, taking the straight road at Larbert Junction, as opposed to previously curving off at Carmuirs West Junction and thence via Linlithgow and the Forth Bridge.*

Opposite: *Meanwhile, six months later, 18th October, No.66134 heads west, skirting the shoreline of the River Forth, approaching Kincardine Bridge with 4J15, the 15:00 Longannet - Hunterston HTA empties. Longannet power station dominates the skyline on the left of view.*

Below: *Meanwhile, on the Stirling - Alloa - Kincardine line itself, No.66183 passes Kincardine East crossing on the final approach to Longannet power station with the inaugural train of loaded coal.* **Guy Houston (3)**

Alloa Opening

Better late than never!

Having originally been due to open in the summer of 2007 - the new line from Stirling to Kincardine, via Alloa, sees the first loaded coal train access the branch bound for Longannet power station on 5th April - No. 66083 hauls this first service, running as 6G18, the 13:00 Hunterston - Longannet.

When the trainplan is fully implemented, operating efficiency will be improved as Longannet can receive coal trains direct, without trains needing to run via the Forth Bridge and Thornton Yard (run round). Plus the more efficient HTA bogie hoppers will replace the incumbent HAAs .

Above: *On Tuesday, 22nd January, No.92029 'Dante' crosses Eynsford Viaduct in Kent with 6B28, Dollands Moor - Wembley 'Silver Bullets', prior to going forward the following day to Mossend and Irvine.* **Alan Hazelden**

Below: *No.66232 is seen passing Inverpeffer (near Arbroath) with 6D83, Laurencekirk - Mossend 'Enterprise' on 12th May, with 'Ermewa' tanks on the the rear to form the 'new to rail' - Aberdeen Waterloo - Blackburn flow of Calcium Carbonate slurry for the Sappi paper mill. This once-weekly flow is in addition to the now well established Waterloo - Irvine flow.* **Jim Ramsay**

CHINA CLAY SLURRY

'Silver Bullets'

EWS start 2008 with the news that the long running 6S55, Burngullow - Irvine flow of china clay slurry ceases but is replaced by a new Channel Tunnel service. The new service originates in Antwerp with the raw material shipped in from South America, before being forwarded by rail to Wembley, thence on to Scotland.

The splendid Class 92s will haul the trains with the slurry conveyed in refurbished ICA bogie tanks, quickly nicknamed 'Silver Bullets' due to their clean and shiny appearance! The first loaded train runs on 9th January when Class 92 No.92002 *H. G. Wells* works north with a rake of 20 ICAs in tow from Wembley to Mossend. The full train plan is as follows:

4431,	22:00	MO	Antwerp - Dollands Moor	4430,	23:20	FO	Dollands Moor - Antwerp
6B28,	10:36	TO	Dollands Moor - Wembley				
6S94,	04:43	WO	Wembley - Mossend	6O60,	05:43	FO	Mossend - Dollands Moor
6R80,	19:14	WO	Mossend - Irvine	6D80,	21:28	ThO	Irvine - Mossend

'Waterloo'

China clay slurry from the Croxton & Garry plant at Waterloo Goods, Aberdeen, is another 'new to rail' freight flow, destined for a paper mill in Darwin, Lancashire; conveyed in ICA tank wagons, the slurry is transported using 'Enterprise' services, although road transport is needed between Blackburn and Darwin, as the Darwin plant is not rail-connected.

Above: *On 13th February, No.92013 'Puccini' passes Beckhouses in Cumbria on the climb to Shap Summit with 6S94, Wembley - Mossend hauling a rake of 20 shiny, loaded loaded ICA tanks.* **Neil Harvey**

Overleaf :

Page 44: *Nicely framed between two Preston-controlled multiple aspect colour light signals, Nos.PN39 and PN41, No.92011 'Handel' heads northwards through Leyland on a rather dank & dismal 16th January with the Antwerp - Irvine loaded china clay slurry tanks, at a time when the ICA tanks were still 'shiny'! This particular leg of the journey is 6S94, the 04:43 (WO) Wembley - Mossend.* **Fred Kerr**

Page 45: *Unfortunately, nothing lasts forever and it's not long before the 'Silver Bullets' lose their shine and become grubby as we see in this view of No 92001 'Victor Hugo' passing Carnforth on 30th April with the northbound 6S94, Wembley - Mossend slurry tanks.* **Andrew Naylor**

FREIGHT FLOWS

EWS NETWORK

Above: EWS is keen to win small freight flows from road, such as the movement of 300 tonnes of bagged seed potato each week from Elgin to Eccles Road during February / March, for cultivation into McCains oven chips. The payload is routed via Mossend and Doncaster using a combination of overnight 'Enterprise' and Intermodal services conveyed in 'Twin' (IZA) 2-axle vans. Eccles Road is about nine miles west of Wymondham on the Ely - Norwich main line and on 4th March, following the arrival of Class 60 No.60018 on 6L99, 09;18 Doncaster - Eccles Road, the bagged seed potato is being unloaded at the Snetterton railhead.   **Iain Scotchman**

Below: 6V62 is certainly a well known train among enthusiasts living in the South West of England; the weekly Fawley to Tavistock Jct. tank train which, at the time of writing, still runs, albeit with no Bitumen traffic due to the closure of the Esso Bitumen depot at Cattewater in May. This is the result of the 40-year old 2-axle TTA Bitumen tanks needing replacement, which is too costly a proposition. The oil carried is traction fuel for Laira and Penzance and the only bitumen traffic from Fawley is now the twice weekly Bromford Bridge flow. Here, in the beautiful Wyle Valley three months earlier on 8th February, No.66250 passes Langford Lakes at the head of 6V62 and a rake of loaded tank wagons - six Bitumen tanks clearly visible behind the locomotive.   **Nic Joynson**

EWS INDUSTRIAL

New Passenger Franchises

Out with the Old .... as November 2007 heralds major changes to the passenger franchise map; farewell Central Trains, GNER, Midland Mainline, Silverlink and Virgin Cross Country, but ....

A Warm Welcome is extended to six new companies:

East Midlands Trains

London Midland,

London Overground,

National Express (East Coast and Anglia)

Arriva Cross Country

South West Trains

Then, as if this isn't enough:

December 2007: Launch of 'Open Access' operator Grand Central, operating HSTs between Sunderland and King's Cross.

April 2008: Wrexham, Shropshire & Marylebone Railway begin running direct passenger trains for the first time in 40 years between Wrexham and London Marylebone using top 'n' tail Class 67s.

Exciting stuff? Let's now have a look at the new train operators who are operating loco-hauled services, plus the trials and tribulations encountered along the way!

Above: *Class 91s running blunt-end first are not an everyday occurence, but on 29th March, the 07:30, Newcastle - London King's Cross is seen passing Hag Lane, Raskelf, with No.91120 leading the train formation in this manner. The days of GNER are over and now* **National Express** *run the prestigious East Coast Main Line passenger services using inherited InterCity 225 electric trainsets and InterCity 125 High Speed Trains. As this view shows, the gold GNER lettering on the Class 91 has disappeared along with the familiar red stripe running along the bodyside of the trainset, which has been replaced with a white bodyside stripe.* **Ian Ball**

National Express East Coast

After 11½ years of successfully running the East Coast franchise, the familiar red stripe livery of GNER has been wiped from the rail network as National Express set out to stamp their own branding on the inherited fleet of rolling stock. And, what better way to advertise your new corporate colours, a film special....

Above: *With snow clad hills in the background, HST power car No.43300 leads 3F00, the Craigentinny - Craigentinny National express East Coast (NXEC) film special over Larbert Viaduct on 9th December 2007.*

Below: *Another view, this time a close up of the train, and No.43238 bringing up the rear of No.43300, passing through Camelon 43 minutes late at 13:43hrs.* **Guy Houston (2)**

Right: *An unidentified southbound HST service overtakes a First Capital Connect Class 313 EMU on a Welwyn Garden City train at Alexandra Palace on 23rd April, with No.43317 in NXEC livery.* **Nick Slocombe**

Overleaf:

Page 50: *A superb composition portraying the Tay Railway Bridge, looking across the water to the 'City of Discovery' - Dundee - famous for jam, jute and journalism! On Monday, 5th May, No.43315 leads a rake of NXEC liveried coaches south over the Tay Bridge forming 1E24, the 14.55 Aberdeen - London King's Cross service.* **Jim Ramsay**

Page 51: *In readiness for the official launch of National Express East Anglia, Class 90 No.90003 'Raedwald of East Anglia' and set NC13 with DVT No.82107 passes Marks Tey, heading for London on 27th February, with 1P33, the 09:30 Norwich - Liverpool Street; the train having been 'stepped-down' from its planned diagram in order to receive a wash and brush up prior to working this service.*

In early 2004, 'One' began replacing their ageing Class 86 locomotives on the Norwich - London route with ex-Virgin Trains Class 90 locomotives; Nos.90001 - 90015 transferred to Norwich Crown Point and, interestingly, No.90003 was also chosen to work the official 'One' launch train between Liverpool Street - Norwich. **James Welham**

Above: *The first Class 91 to receive the new NXEC livery is No.91111, which is seen on 29th July passing Yaxley, to the South of Peterborough, leading 1D41, the 16:35 London King's Cross - Leeds.* **James Welham**

ALL CHANGE

Goodbye 'ONE'....

National Express East Anglia

National Express decide to rebrand all its rail franchises with a single corporate identity.

The Greater Anglia franchise operating as *'ONE'* will become National Express East Anglia. Consequently, the fleet of Class 90 locomotives and Mk. 3 carriages will be re-liveried in the Group's traditional white base and grey livery.

The official launch date for the new National Express East Anglia is 27th February and to mark the occasion a special ceremony takes place at London Liverpool Street; several National Express liveried trains will be present.

Top Right: *On New Year's day, newly reliveried No.90003 'Raedwald of East Anglia' arrives at Ipswich with 1P29, the 11:00 Norwich - Colchester. Raedwald, son of Tytila, was King of the East Angles c600AD - c624AD.* **James Welham**

Above: *Nameplate of No.90003.* **Chris Perkins**

Above: *Prior to receiving the new National Express East Anglia corporate colours, existing locomotives and carriages are being debranded, as illustrated in this image of No.90004 passing through Stratford on 9th February with the 10:00 Norwich - Liverpool Street - will the former 'One' livery be missed?* **Iain Scotchman**

GRAND CENTRAL

Since being formed in 2000, Grand Central has been seeking to operate "open access" rail services for some time. After being unsuccessful with an initial application in 2003 to operate services across the North of England, from Newcastle to Manchester via the Calder Valley, Grand Central re-evaluated the changing requirements and criteria and submitted a detailed and ultimately successful application in 2005 to start services on the Durham Coast between Sunderland and London King's Cross.

Following the statutory period of consultation undertaken by the ORR, Grand Central has been given permission to begin operating passenger services on the Sunderland to London route, with services serving:

Sunderland / Hartlepool / Eaglescliffe / Northallerton / Thirsk / York

There are 6 trains a day on the route, 3 in each direction, commencing Tuesday, 18th December 2007. On the Durham Coast route the key communities of Sunderland, Hartlepool and Eaglescliffe will have direct trains to London for the first time in 20 years, as well as direct links to York and connectional opportunities beyond.

Grand Central will also be seeking a timetable for trains to commence on the Bradford – London route during the timetable that commences in December 2008, with sister company Grand Union seeking to operate on the West Coast Main Line between Euston and Huddersfield / Bradford from 2011.

GRAND CENTRAL TIMETABLE

	Mon - Fri			Saturday			Sunday		
	A								
Sunderland	0646	1230	1730	0653	1230	1730	0910	1342	1842
Hartlepool	0710	1254	1756	0717	1254	1756	0934	1406	1906
Eaglescliffe	0729	1316	1815	0745	1313	1828	0955	1432	1925
Northallerton	0746	1338	1836	0806	1331	1845	1013	1457	1948
Thirsk	0757	1347	1845	0815	1342	1854	1026	1506	1957
York	0822	1410	1906	0847	1405	1916	1047	1531	2015
King's Cross	1032	1605	2108	1045	1602	2117	1251	1730	2220
	B								
King's Cross	0804	1127	1650	0757	1127	1650	0855	1345	1820
York	1014	1322	1847	1000	1330	1852	1054	1553	2025
Thirsk	1030	1338	1905	1021	1351	1921	1110	1610	2042
Northallerton	1039	1347	1916	1032	1409	1930	1121	1620	2051
Eaglescliffe	1058	1405	1934	1049	1427	1950	1140	1640	2118
Hartlepool	1123	1424	2008	1121	1446	2009	1217	1710	2137
Sunderland	1150	1450	2035	1150	1514	2035	1252	1736	2206

A - The Zephyr   **B** - The 21st Century Limited

After the timetable is implemented, Grand Central suffer setbacks due to the poor availability of its HST fleet and have to hire-in locomotives and coaches to fulfill the timetable. Furthermore, effective Wednesday, 21st May, two weekday services each way have to be cancelled altogether and contingency measures set in place whilst its rolling stock undergoes a remedial programme to HST Power Car components to improve reliability. A 'shuttle' service is set up between Sunderland and York to provide alternative rail transport for passengers using stations north of York, rather than rely on road transport, connecting into National Express East Coast services for journey's between there and London.

Above: *Testing commences in November 2007 using a smart looking 7-vehicle HST trainset in black livery with Grand Central branding. No.43080 leads No.43067 passing Thirsk on the East Coast Main Line with 5Z00, Heaton - King's Cross; Grand Central's first test run.* **Ian Ball**

Below: *Journey's end .... No.43084 emerges from Gasworks Tunnel on 30th January heading 1A60, the 06:46 from Sunderland, passing an unsightly block of portakabins standing on the former Cambridge Way stabling point, which once played host to Deltics and the like some 25 years ago!* **Nigel Gibbs**

Above: *'Skips' and Mk.2 stock cover for GCT whilst their own fleet is receiving remedial treatment and on 19th April, No.67026 and No.67020 top 'n' tail 1A62, the 12:30 Sunderland - Kings Cross, seen leaving Hadley Wood Tunnel, running about 10 minutes late.* **Nick Slocombe**

Below. *Due to continuing problems, GCT lay on a shuttle service between Sunderland and York to enable passengers to feed into NXEC services to London. On 16th June, top 'n' tail Class 57/3s No.57308 'Tin Tin' and No.57301 'Scott Tracy' are seen at York with 1Z26, York - Sunderland.* **Guy Houston**

Overleaf: Along the Durham Coast

Page 56: *The Durham Coast presents excellent photgraphic opportunities as these two images demonstrate. Looking back towards Hartlepool Docks, No.43080 leads 1A61, the 13:42 (Sun) Sunderland - King's Cross at Newburn Bridge on 17th February with No.43067 bringing up the rear. The trainset is formed of six carriages sandwiched between the two power cars, which will be the normal formation for these new passenger services.*

Page 57: *On 21st May, one of the GCR contingency 'York Shuttles' (1Z26, the 14:44 York - Sunderland) passes through Hart station with Riviera Trains Class 47/8 No.47815 'Great Western' operating in 'Top 'n' Tail' mode with No.47805 'Talisman'. The chimney stack of the Magnesia works at Cemetry North, Hartlepool, dominates the background.* **Carl Gorse (2)**

Above: *The first train service to run with a complete HST train set in the new East Midlands Trains colours is 1C17, the 07:25 Leeds - London St. Pancras on 2nd May, which is seen passing Pride Parkway, Derby. HST power car No.43048 is leading with No.43058 bringing up the rear.* **Ralf Edge**

Below: *A little while later and 1C17 has arrived at Leicester and is awaiting departure time. This close up view shows off the new, striking, colour scheme on rear power car No.43058, which is alongside Meridian Class 222 DMU No.222020, which also carries striking colours.* **Andy Small**

EAST MIDLANDS TRAINS

East Midlands Trains (EMT) is based in Derby, providing train services in the East Midlands and surrounding areas, principally main line passenger expresses serving the counties of South Yorkshire, Nottinghamshire, Leicestershire and Derbyshire. The franchise is an amalgamation of the former Midland Mainline, which operated inter-city services from London to Derby, Nottingham, Leeds and Sheffield, and the eastern side of Central Trains.

The franchise will run from 11th November 2007 to 1st April 2016 and is legally known as East Midlands Trains Limited; the parent company is Stagecoach Group which also owns South West Trains and 49% of the Virgin Trains franchise. EMT inherits 43 HST power cars.

ARRIVA CROSS COUNTRY

CrossCountry is the brand name of XC Trains Limited, owned by Arriva, which will operate Great Britain's Cross Country rail franchise until April 2016, ostensibly being the former Cross Country franchise held by Virgin Trains. Covering around 1,500 route miles, stretching from Aberdeen to Penzance, and Stansted to Cardiff, this is the most extensive rail network in the UK. The franchise is unusual in that it does not operate any stations, nor has Arriva applied their brand name to the franchise.

Class	Description	No.
43	HST train sets	5
170	Turbostars	29
220	Voyager	34
221	Super Voyager	28

Above: *Cross Country's first refurbished HST power car No.43301 leads the 09:40 Newquay - Newcastle through Worle Parkway on its first weekend in service, Saturday 19th July.* **Chris Perkins**

WREXHAM, SHROPSHIRE & MARYLEBONE RAILWAY

Background: After extensive crew training, open access operator Wrexham, Shropshire & Marylebone Railway (WSMR) start their new service on Monday, 28th April, operating five trains per day in each direction between Wrexham and London Marylebone. So, for the first time since 1967, Wrexham has a direct link to London. WSMR is a joint venture between Renaissance Trains and Deutsche Bahn, the latter having recently taken over Laing Rail (owners of Chiltern Railways and a parent company of WSMR) and EWS, who provide locos. for WSMR.

Route: From Wrexham General, the route runs via Chirk, Ruabon and Gobowen to Shrewsbury, then via Wellington, Telford Central and Cosford to Wolverhampton. From Wolverhampton, the route has the major obstacle of Birmingham to circumvent and is routed via Tame Bridge Parkway, then non-stop via Birmingham International, Coventry and Leamington Spa, before joining the Chiltern Main Line at Banbury.

Rolling Stock: Each of the daily services will be hauled by top 'n' tail EWS Class 67s. Four locomotives (Nos.67012 to 67015) have been allocated for WSMR work and repainted in two-tone silver/metallic grey livery. Later in the year, trains will comprise a DVT along with a single Class 67 at the south end of the train. Carriages for WSMR were still being refurbished by Marcroft by the time the new operation went live, so the Company use a MK.3 set hired from Cargo-D in the interim. There are three train sets in use, formed of two TSOs and a RFM restaurant vehicle, which will be serviced at Crewe Electric depot and Chiltern's Wembley depot.

Crew Training: From February, intensive crew training takes place with two sets being utilised; one on the northern stretch between Wrexham and Wolverhampton and a second set running between Banbury and Marylebone. For route learning around the West Midlands suburbs, Chiltern Railways departmental Class 121 'bubble car' has been been commandeered for this purpose!

WSMR Timetable - Weekdays:

Wrexham to London	1P01	1P03	1P13	1P33	1P65
Wrexham General	0542	0725	1110	1510	1810
Ruabon	0549	0732	1117	1517	1817
Chirk	0555	0739	1123	1523	1823
Gobowen	0600	0744	1128	1528	1828
Shrewsbury	0625	0810	1153	1553	1853
Wellington		0823	1205	1606	1906
Telford Central	0642	0829	1211	1612	1912
Cosford	0650	0837	1220	1620	1920
Wolverhampton			1232s	1632s	1934s
Tame Bridge Parkway	0715	0912	1243	1643	1948
Banbury	0833s	1025s	1402s	1802s	2101s
London Marylebone	0954	1149	1523	1922	2215

London to Wrexham	1J80	1J81	1J82	1J83	1J84
London Marylebone	0645	1017	1317	1610	2003
Banbury	0800u	1129u	1430u	1731u	2114u
Tame Bridge Parkway	0906	1242	1539	1841	2223
Wolverhampton	0925u	1255u	1555u		2236u
Cosford	0940	1307	1607	1907	2247
Telford Central	0951	1315	1615	1915	2256
Wellington		1321	1621	1921	
Shrewsbury	1012	1342	1638	1941	2315
Gobowen		1407	1704	2007	2336
Chirk	1050	1412	1709	2012	2341
Ruabon	1056	1419	1716	2019	2348
Wrexham General	1044	1428	1725	2028	2357

Notes:

s - set down only   **u** - pick up only

Four trains operate each way on Saturdays at different times from the Weekdays timetable and three services on Sundays, which utilise three sets of stock.

Finally, these new services offer railway photographers exciting new possibilities on routes unaccustomed to loco-hauled passenger activity. A comprehensive selection of training runs and actual service trains are included overleaf, prior to the introduction of DVTs. Apologies if the take up seems a little OTT, but who knows what the future will bring!

Above: *Wrexham & Shropshire branding on a WSMR Class 67 locomotive.*   **Mark Riley**

Opposite: *From 22nd April, a full "Shadow" timetable is introduced for 7-days until the official start of passenger services and on the 22nd, No.67012 with No.67014 at the rear, heads another day's staff training special and is passing Banbury Stone Terminal.*   **Ian Ball**

5Z63

Above: *Intensive crew training takes place from February until the WSMR timetbale comes into effect on 28th April. On the morning of 21st February, the 'Up' crew training special sits in the loop at Banbury station prior to departing with 5Z63, a VSTP working to Hinksey Yard and return. Class 67 No.67016 will head the train south and No.67017 (DIT on rear and out of view) will take over for the return journey.*

Opposite: *Meanwhile, on 27th March, No.67024 is topping the train and No.67003 is tailing, 5Z63, the 08:33 Banbury - Marylebone WSMR training run, having just emerged from the short Brill Tunnel. The date on the tunnel is 1909, the Bicester cut-off line was not opened by the GWR until 1910.* **Geoff Plumb (2)**

Princes Risborough

Above: *The first southbound working of the "real" services operated by WSMR takes place on Monday, 28th April, and 1P01, 05:42 from Wrexham to Marylebone, is unfortunately dogged by problems; 15 minutes late departing Wrexham due to a brakes problem and 25 minutes late arriving at Wellington. The leading engine, No.67025 'Western Star', fails at this point and No.67026 is taken off the rear of the train and installed at the head, reaching Wolverhampton 57 minutes late. Still with the two locos on the front, but now only 38 minutes late, the train is seen arriving at Princes Risborough at 09:48 en route to Marylebone.*

Below: *Same location, different era, and the last day semaphore signalling was in operation, parts of the signals having already been removed and the new colour light signalling is in place, but yet to be commissioned. At the time, most services were operated by Class 115 DMUs, but these were on their last legs and there was a shortage of sets. So, some services were worked by Class 47s and Mk.I coaches, such as on 1st March 1991 when Network South East-liveried Class 47/4 No.47521 arrived with the 14:51, Aylesbury - London Marylebone.* **Geoff Plumb (2)**

Above: *Nos.67014 and 67013 top 'n' tail 5Z63, the 08:33 Banbury - Marylebone training and is the first run involving WSMR liveried locos, which are seen approaching Ashendon Junction on the lovely morning of Wednesday, 9th April it is a shame the puddle is not a bit larger!* **Geoff Plumb**

Below: *This is train 1P50, Ruabon - London Paddington, diverted to Paddington because of various engineering works on Sunday, 21st September, and a strange formation of two sets coupled together. The second train is removed at Crewe, whereupon it runs to Chester and back and then ECS to Shrewsbury mid-afternoon. The two top 'n' tail sets comprising Nos.67013 + 67025 and Nos.67026 + 67019, respectively, are seen negotiaiting Sutton Bank, Rednal. Although it makes a good shot, it screws up all the rest of the working for the day!* **Ian Ball**

Above: Class 67 No.67015 'David J. Lloyd' is on the rear of 1J80, while No.67028 is leading as they head north at 07:31 with the 06:45 Marylebone - Wrexham, as a Chiltern Clubman heads south with the 06:53 from Banbury. Seen from the bow girder bridge on the A4129 near Kingsey on Monday, 19th May.

Below: The southern part of the Wrexham & Shropshire crew training runs takes place between Banbury and Marylebone and on 5th March, the afternoon working (5Z23, 14:02 ex-Banbury) approaches the remains of Ardley station, with No.67002 'Special Delivery' at the head and No.67017 'Arrow' dead on the rear.   **Geoff Plumb (2)**

Above: *Away we go .... on 7th May, WSMR-liveried No.67012 leaves Wrexham with 1P13, the 11:10 Wrexham General - London Marylebone, in hazy sunshine and humid May weather; No.67014 is DIT on the rear.*

Below: *Mixed liveries .... WSMR No.67014 and EWS No.67028, running in top 'n' tail formation, are seen the previous day from Tal-y-Cafn Woods on Cefn Viaduct, which spans the River Dee, with 1P33, the 15:10 Wrexham General - London Marylebone; a lovely setting on a beautiful late Spring afternoon.* **Mark Riley (2)**

Above: *There are some great photographic locations to be found in Shropshire, such as Chirk Viaduct on the 'Didcot & Chester' Line (Anglo-Welsh border), where Nos.67012 & 67024 are seen on 6th May, working a three-coach 1P13, the 11:10 Wrexham General - London Marylebone.* **Mark Riley**

Below: *On 9th June, No.67025 works 1J81, the 10:17 Marylebone - Wrexham WSMR service and is seen passing the former Walcot Sugar Beet factory. The factory, having dominated the Shropshire sky line for many years, is being demolished and very soon will be nothing but a memory.* **Mike Hemming**

Above: On Saturday, 30th August, No.67012 (No.67024 DIT rear) passes the Kronospan factory on the approach to Chirk station with 1P33, the 15:10 Wrexham General - London Marylebone; Kronospan being the largest wood-panel manufacturer in the UK and part of the largest global wood-panel manufacturing group. — **Mark Riley**

Below: The previous day, EWS-liveried Nos.67028 + 67019 (DIT) are seen working 1J81, the 10:17 Marylebone - Wrexham across Chirk Viaduct, alongside the Llangollen canal aqueduct, both crossing the Afon Ceiriog, marking the border between England (on the far side) and Wales. The railway viaduct is 100 feet high and has 10 spans, standing some 30 feet above the aqueduct, which carries the canal 70 feet above the river for a distance of 710 feet. — **Geoff Plumb**

HULL TRAINS

Arise Sir William ....

The eagerly awaited operation of the AC Locomotive Group's Class 86/1 No.86101 *Sir William A Stanier FRS* with Hull Trains commences 11th January following successful commissioning and training runs. Used with DVT No.82115, the 'Push-Pull' trainset consists of five Cargo-D Mk. 3 vehicles with the Class 86/1 locomotive positioned at the London end of the formation, which is contrary to normal ECML running. The Mk. 3 vehicles are:

TSO : 12043 / 12014 / 12038   RMB : 10202   TF : 11031

The Hull Trains loco-hauled diagram is:

Fridays   : 5G97 13:34 Bounds Green - Doncaster
             1G97 20:20 Doncaster - King's Cross

Saturdays   : 1G03 09:34 King's Cross - Doncaster
             1G97 19:10 Doncaster - King's Cross

Sundays   : 1G02 10:42 King's Cross - Doncaster
             5G02 12:33 Doncaster - Bounds Green

Above: *A close up view of No.86101 'on the blocks' at King's Cross on 9th February upon arrival with 1G97, the 19:10 service from Doncaster. After 40 years WCML running, who'd have expected a 'Can' on the East Coast?*

Top Right: *On 19th January, Porterbrook DVT (No.82115), finished in 'rail blue' following overhaul at Marcroft, Stoke, leads 1G03, the 09:34 (SO) ex-King's Cross into Doncaster with 'Sir William' bringing up the rear.*

Bottom Right: *After the passengers detrain from 1G03, No.86101 is seen positioning the ECS at Doncaster, which will be stabled and prepared for the 19:10hrs (1G97) service to King's Cross.* **Carl Gorse (3)**

Overleaf :

Page 74: *The train plan for Friday and Sunday involve ECS moves between Doncaster and London. On 17th February, No.86101 is seen heading south at Retford with ECS, running on this occasion as 5G42, Doncaster - Bounds Green.* **Mick Tindall**

Page 75: *On 16th February, No.86101 propels a late-running 1G03, 09:34 King's Cross - Doncaster through Brookmans Park, just over 14 miles into its journey.* **Iain Scotchman**

A 'Mentor' Case: *Thursday, 24th January, provides the very rare sight of Class 31s on the 'Mentor' test train North of the Border and, even better, is its multi-coloured nature, seen passing a rather old church amidst a sea of industrial work units on the approach to Paisley. The Mainline Rail pairing of No.31454 'The Heart of Wessex' + No.31601 'Guage O Guild 1956 - 2006' top 'n' tail 1Q18, Polmadie - Polmadie circular via Largs.* **Guy Houston**

A Breath of Fresh Air *.... would surely be appreciated by local residents as we see No.31454 again, but this time six days later, passing through Stockton with a barrier coach sandwiched between the 'Goyle' and Advenza Class 47 No.47237, running as 5Z76, Stockton - Wensleydale.* **Carl Gorse**

Tendring 'Goyles': *On 5th June, Class 31s No.31190 and No.31459 top 'n' tail test coach No.DB999508 as they accelerate through Kirby Cross with 2Q08, Ipswich CSD - Walton on Naze Serco test train.* **Iain Scotchman**

Three's Company: *While waiting the passage of freight trains on the Birmingham - Derby main line at Portway on 26th June, the cameraman has the bonus of seeing purple liveried Class 31 No.31601 'Guage O Guild 1956 - 2006' + Network Rail Nos.31205 + 31123 triple-heading a Gloucester - Derby RTC NMT.* **Fred Kerr**

CELEBRITY 'TUGS'

It is probably fair to say, that apart from Class 37s, the other traction which captivates the rail enthusiast audience at the present time is Class 60s. Even more so now, as EWS have decided to relivery some class members (perhaps as a result of the new tie up with DNB Schenker) and commemorate some notable organisations in the process.

To begin with, and to honour the work carried out by the Teenage Cancer Trust, Class 60 No.60074 receives a new coat of light blue paint and is adorned with the Trust's logo. The paint job is carried out at Toton and No.60074 moves to the National Railway Museum (NRM) at York for a special naming & unveiling ceremony on St. David's Day, Saturday, 1st March.

Hot on its heels, No.60040 is "In the Army now" .... the British Army's territorial arm is celebrating its Centenary and EWS finishes the loco in all-over maroon, sporting 'British Army - Be The Best - Regular & Territorial' branding. It is named *'The Territorial Army Centenary'* by HRH Duke of York on 14th June, also at the NRM, York.

The movements of these particular locomotives and other Class 60s are eagerly followed by cameramen the length and breadth of the network and a small selection of their photographic exploits are included for your enjoyment.

Above: *There are two ex-Mainline blue liveried 'tugs' - No.60007 and No.60044 - and it is the former loco which is pictured in charge of 6D07, the 05:54 Warrington Arpley - Sinfin on 13th March, heading east through Willington, seen from a footpath off Etwall Road near the Level Crossing. The consist is seven 100 ton bogie petroleum tanks conveying Avgas for Rolls Royce from Grangemouth oil refinery.* **Ralf Edge**

Previously :   **A 'LICKEY' EXPERIENCE**

Page 78: *Overnight snow, followed by a bright clear start to the day, produce superb conditions in which to record this working of the Network Rail Test Train en route from Derby RTC to Bristol Barrow Hill on Sunday, 6th April, running as 4Z08. With the unique Wessex Trains liveried Class 31/6 No.31601 'Gauge 'O' Guild 1956-2006' leading, the colourful combination descends the Lickey Incline at speed, No.31233 is at the rear of the formation. The Test Train is due to cover lines in the West of England, visiting both Plymouth and Minehead.*

Page 79: *At the end of 2007, the long running Burngullow - Irvine china clay service ceases, being replaced by a new working from Antwerp, Belgium, conveying slurry imported from Brazil. There remained the supply of china clay from Cornwall to the Potteries, which is normally routed via Newport and Hereford to Bescot, with Class 66 traction being the norm. However, on Saturday, 12th April, engineering work in Severn Tunnel required the overnight 6M55 service from Tavistock Junction to be routed via Cheltenham and, as EWS had allocated a Class 60 locomotive, a rare opportunity presents itself to photograph a Class 60 hauled china clay train being banked up the Lickey Incline. Photographed near Finstall, Class 60 No.60048 'Eastern' makes light work of the 11 loaded JIA Covhops and 2 bogie vans with the assistance of a Class 66 at the rear.* **Don Gatehouse**

Above: *Nameplate* 'Teenage Spirit' *applied to No.60074*　　　　　　**Carl Gorse**

Above: '*Teenager Cancer Trust' branding applied to the bodyside of No.60074*　　　　**Ralf Edge**

Below: *Inside the National Rail Museum, No.60074 shows off the new livery, which incorporates DB Schenker branding, the German parent company of EWS. At the ceremony, Guest of Honour, Mr. Chris Chittel, presents a cheque for £250,000 to the Trust, which will go towards a new cancer unit at St. James hospital, Leeds.*

Carl Gorse

LOCOMOTIVE GALLERY

Above: *On Wednesday 5th March, following the launch at the NRM on the 1st, No.60074 makes its second appearance on the Lindsey - Westerleigh tanks as recorded in this panoramic view at Westerleigh oil terminal, preparing to depart with 6E41, the 10:42 empties bound for Lindsey.* **Chris Perkins**

Top Right: *On Friday, 15th August, No.60040 is rostered to work 6M81, Margam - Round Oak steel, accelerating its heavy train past a lower quadrant semaphore signal approaching Droitwich Spa station.* **Peter Tandy**

Bottom Right: *On the penultimate day of July, No.60074 passes Ramsey Road, Whittlesea, with a mix of 'Cemex' branded HOA and debranded RMC JGA bogie hoppers forming 6L73, Peak Forest - Ely.* **John Rudd**

Below: *For several days in July, No.60040 works out of Acton Yard on local 'trips' to stone terminals in Kent, such as on 17th July when seen passing Aylesford with 6Y17, Allington - Hither Green empty JHA bogie hoppers. This service will travel via the Medway Valley line to Strood, Hoo Junction, Dartford, Lee spur and into Hither Green from the north, where it will join up with another empty stone train, normally the Ardingly - Hither Green, to form a 'jumbo' train working back to Whatley Quarry.* **Alan Hazelden**

Above: *The Leeds - Skipton line does not receive a great deal of photographic coverage, which is a pity as the Yorkshire Dales is a beautiful part of the country, as this view clearly shows. On 19th March, No.60074 'Teenage Spirit' passes Cononley with 6E13, Newbiggin - Milford empty Gypsum containers.*
Neil Harvey

Below: *A popular photographic location on the GWML between Didcot and Swindon is Denchworth, where an overbridge on a minor road leading from the main A417 Faringdon to Wantage road, gives unrestricted views in both directions. Looking east towards Didcot on Thursday afternoon, 14th August, No.60040 'The Territorial Army Centenary' is in charge of 6B33, Theale - Robeston petroleum empties comprising a mix of VTG and Tiphook TDA and TEA wagons.*
Martin Buck

60007

Above: *This particular 'Tug', along with No.60059, still retains the striking Loadhaul colours and their movements are closely monitored by railway photgraphers. On 29th July, the cameraman has the bonus of No.60040 'The Territorial Army Centenary' being moved back to Humberside behind No.60059, seen passing Avenue Bridge, Newsham, near Thirsk, with 6D11, Lackenby - Scunthorpe steel empties.* **Ian Ball**

60059 *'Swinden Dalesman'*

Below: *The 'unbeastied' No.60059 pulls away from a crew change at Stourton, Leeds, on 12th July with 6D76, Redcar - Rylstone loaded limestone, formed of NACCO JGA covered bogie hoppers.* **Neil Harvey**

Above: *The cement trains from Tunstead to both Walsall and Willesden run alternate Tuesdays and utilise hopper-based bogie tanks, unusually classified under a JGA TOPS code. The returning empties provide the best photographic opportunities, as we see here with No.60059 heading north through Stenson Junction (Heath Lane, Findern) on 12th July with 6M82, Walsall - Tunstead.* **Ralf Edge**

Below: *Meanwhile, in East Anglia on 21st July, No.60059 passes Australia Farm Crossing, March, leading 6M87, Ely Potter Group - Peak Forest formed of a mixed rake of 24 hoppers (ex-RMC 'JGAs' and newer Cemex 'HOAs'). The train is running about 40 minutes behind schedule approaching the quiet, gated, crossing.* **James Welham**

LOCOMOTIVE GALLERY

A FRESH COAT of PAINT
FGW

Above: *First Great Western (FGW) decide to repaint its fleet of Class 57/6s in the same colour as the HST fleet, blue, but minus 'Neon Tubes'. The work is carried out at Brush Barclay and on 27th March, No.57605 'Totnes Castle' returns home, running as 0Z57, Kilmarnock - Old Oak Common, passing Carnforth.* **Andrew Naylor**

Below: *Heading into the summer months, No.57604 'Pendennis Castle' has the distinction of being the sole remaining FGW Class 57/6 locomotive in Great Western Green livery. On 10th June, she is seen heading 1C99, the 23:50 London Paddington - Penzance 'Night Riviera' service across Hayle's Foundry Square. The sleeping cars do, however, look smart, following their reburfishment and re-livery at Wolverton.* **James Welham**

47832

Opposite: *Between February and May, Class 47/8 No.47832 metamorphoses from Victa Westlink colours to Stobart Rail livery and these three images, all shot at Carnforth, show the transition.* **Andrew Naylor (3)**

Previously:

Page 88: *On Tuesday, 4th March, No.60030 crosses Ceirog Valley at Chirk with 6V75, Dee Marsh - Margam steel empties, below which is Thomas Telford's magnificent aquaduct carrying the Shropshire Union Canal. Two fine examples of Victorian civil engineering still in use today.* **John Binch**

Page 89: *One of the author's favourites. A reminder of the only current freight flow to use 'hooded' 2-axle HBA, HCA and HNA MGR-style hoppers; Limestone trains from Hardendale & Shap quarries to Lackenby & Redcar steelworks. On 12th March, No.60013 heads from the 'Up' main onto the 'Up' goods line at Whitehouse Junction, Cargo Fleet, with 6N92, Redcar - Tees Yard limestone empties; a portion for 6M46 to Hardendale.* **Ian Ball**

Before

During

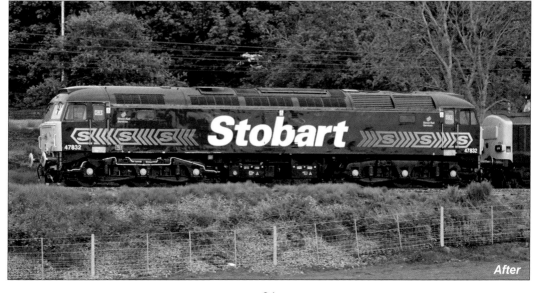

After

LOCOMOTIVE GALLERY

47760

Above: *Acquired by West Coast Railway Company (WCRC) in 2007, ex-EWS Class 47/7 No 47760 returns to main line running, wearing WCRC maroon livery and fitted with snowploughs. On 31st May, No 47760 is seen working vice failed No.50049 on 1Z52, the 08:18 Kings Cross - York (outward diesel hauled leg of return steam charter with A4 Pacific No.60007) at speed on the 'Down Fast' line passing Tempsford.* **Nigel Gibbs**

Below: *Past and present at Carlisle on 24th May with No.47760 stabled alongside fellow WCRC Class 8f 2-8-0 No.48151, both of which featuring on Railtourer's 1Z49, Hull - Carlisle 'Settle & Carlisle Discovery Steam Special', although the headbord carried by the 8f is entitled 'Settle & Carlisle Thunderer'! It is quite fitting to include a picture of an 8f, being one of the classes of steam locomotive to soldier on in the North West of England until the end of steam in 1968 - 40 years ago, but still fresh in the memory of many an enthusiast.* **Richard Jones**

Airshow Special

Above: *Advenza Class 47 No.47375 is called upon to work one of the 'specials' laid on in conjunction with the airshow at Lowestoft beach during 24th & 25th July. On the first day, No.47375 heads past the semaphores and signal box at Oulton Broad North with 1G92, the 09:48 Norwich - Lowestoft.* **Nic Joynson**

Scarborough Spa Express

Above: *Class 47/4 No.47826 is rebranded at Carnforth on 15th July for an innovative advertising campaign to promote the 'Scarborough Spa Express' steam specials, operated by WCRC, which run during the summer months between York and Scarborough via Harrogate and Leeds. The locomotive is stabled at York, where it is used as a 'Thunderbird' and shunting engine, as is the case on 14th August.* **Carl Gorse**

An Odd Couple ....

Above: *On Thursday, 14th May, 6Z72, the 10:25 Stockton - Cardiff Tidal scrap metal working is rostered for Advenza Class 57 No. 57006 but, between Derby and Gloucester, the Class 57 is joined by Class 47/4 No.47818 'Emily' and the unusual combination is recorded passing Bromsgrove with 14 KEA bogie box wagons in tow. The Class 47 still carries the remnants of its former 'One' colours.* **Don Gatehouse**

Stoneblowing

Middle: *On 25th March, No.57009 hauls the Stoneblower along the ECML 'Up Slow' line at New Southgate, running as 6Z11, the 09:30 Doncaster Marshgate - Ashford.*
Nigel Gibbs

Left: *When there is a Stoneblower move, more often than not it's just the one loco on the front and normally a Class 37, so getting a pair of Class 57s is quite rare. On 19th May, Nos. 57009 + 57010 double-head 6Z57, Ashford - Wymondham Stoneblower, at Tonbridge.* **Alan Hazelden**

Operation *'Refresh'*

Above: *FGW launched this refurbishment programme in January 2007 - HST Power cars at Loughborough and coaching stock at Derby. As this nears completion, associated moves cease to be a regular day to day feature with freight operators providing a variety of motive power for these workings. On 25th January, Advenza's No.47237 passes Stoke Prior with refurbished stock, running as 5Z91, Derby - Plymouth Laira.* **Don Gatehouse**

STOCK MOVES

Continental 'Mega 3s'

Above: *The entire fleet of 22 KAA Mega 3 'Pocket' wagons have been sold to NACCO for intermodal use on behalf of Rail Link Europe. On a dull & dank 1st February, Colas Rail Class 47/7 No.47727 'Rebecca' is passing Highworth Junction, Swindon,* taking the KAAs *on the first leg of their journey to the Continent, running as 6Z01, Aberthaw - Dollands Moor. The KAAs have been reclassified IXAs in the RIV 37.80.4905 series.* **Martin Buck**

Above: *Long Marston has seen some odd-looking trains in recent years, but this must take the biscuit for the oddest. Nos.66722 + 66724 arrive from Leeds with a single FLHH hopper on Friday, 13th June, but it is the return 4Z89 working to Crewe which is the real focus of interest. No.87002 'Royal Sovereign' was due to be taken out prior to a loaded test run the following week, but to see such a mixed train is a real surprise. Here, No.66722 'Sir Edward Watkin' with No.87002, a Cargo-D Mk3, and 3 FLHH hoppers tailed by No.66724 'Drax Power Station' leave Honeybourne East Loop and join the Cotswold Line to head for Evesham, Worcester and Crewe.*

Below: *A pair of HNRC Class 20s see some activity on Tuesday, 8th January, when Nos.20905 + 20901 take four Arriva-liveried coaches from Crewe to Long Marston. The train, reporting code 5Z90, is seen arriving in the platform at Honeybourne, much to the bemusement of the solitary passenger waiting for his train south!* **Peter Tandy (2)**

Above: *No.20905 is seen again, when on hire to Cotswold Rail, spending a week or so in Craigentinny waiting to return a repaired Grand Central HST power car to its home depot at Heaton. This move duly happens on 14th August (5Z50, Craigentinny - Heaton) with the ensemble going via Edinburgh Waverley & Haymarket in order to keep the 20 pointing the right way. The Class 20 + No.43068 is passing through Haymarket at 10:15hrs (3 late) heading west, before turning east and going around the south suburban line.*

Below: *Another Advenza ECS move but, this time, No.47828 'Joe Strummer' taking translator vehicles (for use in Class 318 / 320 overhauls) to Glasgow Works and three Mk2D coaches up to Inverness. On 19th August, No.47828 is seen on 5Z60 Gloucester - Glasgow Works, waiting for the road at Springburn and the short run to Eastfield, where the 47 will run round for the last leg of the journey.* **Guy Houston (2)**

The 'Praxis Express'

Above: *In May, First GBRf launch the 'Praxis Express', aimed at train owners looking to transport wagons to / from Praxis Engineering's workshop in Long Marston, Warwickshire, running two train services per week. The 'Praxis Express' can be diverted off route if necessary to deliver or pick up vehicles, which need to be tested or stored before onward travel. On Tuesday, 20th May, 'Medite' No.66709 'Joseph Arnold Davies', passes Bromsgrove with eight FHH hoppers, running as 6Z87, Leeds - Long Marston.*

Hired Help!

Below: *Having secured a contract to deliver coal from Daw Mill Colliery to Ratcliffe Power Station, Fastline run the inaugural service on 12th May but, pending the arrival of their own Class 66/3 locomotives, a First GBRF Class 66/7 is hired as an interim measure. At the commencement of the second week, No.66724 passes Washwood Heath at the head of the loaded 6D00 service from Daw Mill.* **Don Gatehouse (2)**

Above: *Pending a further batch of new locomotives, Freightliner Heavy Haul hire DRS Class 66/4s to satisfy their freight obligations, such as in March, to cover the two diagrams on the Boulby branch. The first image depicts No.66423 leaving Tees Dock heading for Grangetown loop on 4th March, where the locomotive will run round before going forward with 6F33, the 12:43 Tees Dock - Boulby Potash empties.*

Below: *Meanwhile, earlier in the day, sister locomotive No.66425 sweeps round the curve at Redcar, passing Coatham Marsh nauture reserve, with 6F32, the 09:34 Boulby Mine - Tees Dock loaded Potash. The consist is made up entirely of three designs of covered bogie hoppers. For example:*

> *1st wagon : JIA (33.70.0894.100-152 series)*
> *2nd wagon : JGA (NACO 17450-17456 series)*
> *4th wagon : JGA (NACO 19250-19280 series)*

The above wagon types convey Rock Salt as well as Potash.　　　　　　　　　　　　　　　　　　**Carl Gorse (2)**

LOCOMOTIVE GALLERY

NEW 'GRIDS' on the BLOCK

56311

Above: *The first 'Grid' to be resurrected by Hanson Traction and to re-enter traffic is the ex-No.56057, becoming No.56311, on behalf of Fastline, which is rather timely as the current batch of Fastline 'Grids (Nos.56301 - 56303) have been out of traffic at some point. On 5th June, No.56311 heads No.56301 on 4E90, Thamesport - Doncaster intermodal, passing Horninglow Street, Burton-on-Trent; '301 having failed earlier in the week and is being towed around the country for a couple of days before being repaired.* **Ralf Edge**

Below: *Meanwhile, a splash of summer colours makes up for the rather drab, grey, livery worn by No.56311, which is seen passing Lea Marston on 11th June with a fully laden 4O90, Birch Coppice - Thamesport.* **Dave Stracey**

56312

Above: *From the sublime to the ridiculous, or vice versa depending on your point of view. Ex-Loadhaul No.56003 has been overhauled at Wansford on the Nene Valley Railway, Peterborough, to become No.56312 and repainted in purple livery with the branding 'Artemis' applied to the bodyside. It remains to be seen what degree of success Hanson Traction's entrepreneur, Garcia Hanson, has in the locomotive 'spot hire' market.* **Michael Wright**

56313

Below: *And the next one? It is proposed No.56128 will follow (becoming No.56313), which is seen inside the shed at Wansford on 3rd August, while in the process of being prepared for eventual main line return.* **Richard Jones**

LOCOMOTIVE GALLERY

1998 - 2008

To mark the 10th Anniversary of the Class 66 locomotive, a special commemorative cover is produced for the Autumn 2008 edition of 'Freightmaster'. It features one example from previous editions for each of the four freight operators who were using Class 66s on the 10th Anniversary, 18th April 2008:

Top Left: *Issue 25 - EWS No.66163 passing Beckfoot with 6Z27, Ayr - Ironbridge power station loaded MGR, running on this occasion in the path of 6M40 to Rugeley.*

Top Right: *Issue 27 - FHH No.66603 heads through Burton on Trent with 6E55, Kingsbury - Humber and a distinctive, uniform, rake of empty blue petroleum TEA bogie wagons.*

Bottom Left: *Issue 34 - GBRf No.66708 at Eastleigh on 6Y19, Mountfield - Southampton Western Docks empty Gypsum containers*

Bottom Right: *Issue 41 - DRS No.66408 on 4R77, Grangemouth - Elderslie intermodal at Greenfoot.*

Martin Buck (4)

2008 marks the 10th Annivesary of the Class 66 locomotive in the UK.

On 18th April 1998, the first Class 66 (ordered by EWS) arrives at Immingham, having been shipped across the Atlantic Ocean from Albany, New York, in the hold of Dutch-registered MV *'Fairload'* - No.66001 being the first in a consignment of 250 from General Motors. The EWS Class 66s soon have a virtual monopoly of freight services throughout the UK and, christened 'Sheds' by rail enthusiasts, become the universal freight locomotive across the network, thus removing any problems of traction knowledge among train crews. Of course, from an enthusiast perspective, this is potentially bad news, as they gradually replace classic traction on freight flows.

Other freight operators soon follow suit and order their own fleet of Class 66s, fortunately with corporate liveries more pleasing on the eye than the EWS Maroon & Gold. At the time of closing for print, this is the state of play:

Class 66 Liveries

Operator	Number Range	Livery
EWS	66001 - 66250	Maroon bodyside & roof with broad gold bodyside band
	A batch has been converted for use in France. They have lost their EWS logo in favour of Euro Cargo Rail branding, the addition of chevrons on their front, but retaining the EWS colours.	
Fastline	66301 - 66305	Grey and black with yellow and white stripes
DRS	66401 - 66434	Dark blue with 'Compass' markings
	66411	Stobart Rail
	66412	Malcolm
Freightliner	66501 - 66625	Dark green with yellow cabs
	66522	Shanks Waste - one half of loco in Shanks' Waste light green
	66623	Bardon Aggregates
	66951 - 66957	Dark green with yellow cabs
GBRf	66701 - 66717	Blue with orange cantrail & solebar stripes, orange cabs
	66705	Golden Jubilee 'Union Jack'
	66709	Medite
	66718 - 66722	Metronet
	66723 - 66732	First Group

'Billy Bolsover'

Above: *Resplendent, Class 66/6 No.66623 passes through Lincoln with 6M00, Humber - Kingsbury loaded petroleum TEA bogie tanks on 7th December 2007. During the official opening of subsidiary company London Concrete's new Watford terminal on 16th November 2007, the locomotive is named 'Billy Bolsover' after the Chief Executive of Aggregate Industries.* **Guy Houston**

66405 - First and Last

Above: . *Effective 6th September, the 'Tesco Express' is scheduled to run on a sixth day (Saturday) and it is somewhat surprising that No.66405 and not No.66412 (see opposite), nor indeed No.66411, is diagrammed to haul the inaugural 4Z43, 06:31 Daventry - Grangemouth, which is seen heading north through Camelon station with a rake of distinctive Tesco 'LessCO$_2$' branded containers trailing in its wake.* **Guy Houston**

Below: *On 28th March, Direct Rail Services announce their intention to relinquish the first 10 members from its Class 66/4 locomotive fleet during 2008, following the expiry of a contract with the leasing company - one being the original W.H.Malcolm dedicated locomotive, No.66405. In truly appalling weather, No.66405 heads south at Carnforth on 14th October with 4M44, Mossend - Daventry 'Malcolm' intermodal and it is No.66405's final appearance for DRS as it, along with Nos.66401-66404, goes 'off lease' the following day.* **Andrew Naylor**

Malcolm Rail

Above: *This is the new look for 'Malcolm Rail' as DRS unveil a new livery on No.66412, which is carrying a striking black and blue version of W.H.Malcolm's new corporate livery. The previous colours were worn by dedicated 'Dred' No.66405 and the new colour scheme is seen to good effect in the above image of No.66412 passing Carnforth with 4Z34, the 05:00 Coatbridge - Daventry on 17th September, running 35-minutes behind schedule at this point in the journey.* **Andrew Naylor**

Severn Crossing

Overleaf: *A delightful setting and Class 66/0 No.66109 slowly crossing the River Severn on 27th February with a rake of empty HTA bogie coal hoppers, running as 4F59, Ironbridge power station - Walton Old Junction.*

The Albert Edward Bridge at Coalbrookdale in Shropshire opened on 1st November 1864 and its design is almost identical to the Victoria Bridge which carries the Severn Valley Railway over the River Severn between Arley and Bewdley in Worcestershire. Designed by John Fowler, it has a 200-foot span cast iron arch, originally built to carry the Severn Junction Railway across the river, it now carries power station coal traffic to Ironbridge, accessed from Madeley Junction on the Wolverhampton - Shrewsbury main line. **Mike Hemming**

BRITAIN'S BEST JOIN FORCES

Rail freight's biggest British-owned haulier and Royal Air Force squadrons from RAF Odiham come together on Tuesday, 2nd September, to officially name a First GBRf Class 66 locomotive *'Chinook"* at First GBRf's depot at Finedon Road, Wellingborough. Station Commander at RAF Odiham, Group Captain Andy Turner OBE, and the rest of his crew fly a Chinook into the depot to begin the proceedings and, as the aircraft approaches the landing site, the crowd are treated to a short demonstration of the helicopter's capability.

Following the arrival of the aircraft, Group Captain Turner and John Smith, Managing Director of First GBRf, unveil the name plaque on loco No.66723 at the ceremony. John Smith says: "It's a real pleasure for me to be able to perform this naming ceremony. We owe a huge debt of gratitude to the brave service men and women who serve in areas of conflict like Afghanistan and at First GBRf we wanted to demonstrate our respect for their outstanding commitment and professionalism by naming a loco in their honour."

Station Commander, Group Captain Andy Turner, responds: "We are delighted that First GBRf have decided to name their loco *'Chinook'*. It is an appropriate name as the aircraft is synonymous with heavy lifting and freight movement and it is fantastic to be recognised for what we do in Afghanistan." As well as operating duties in Afghanistan, RAF Odiham perform a number of other duties using the Chinook helicopter. In recent years the Chinook has been used to aid the hostage rescue in Sierra Leone; to move food, water, blankets and tents to remote mountain locations after the Pakistan earthquake; the aircraft also helped with flood prevention and relief around Gloucestershire and Yorkshire during last years floods.

Also in attendance at the event are aircrew from No 7,18 and 27 Squadrons of the RAF, who are responsible for flying Chinook helicopters, as well as First GBRf employees.

Left: *The Chinook makes for an impressive sight as it entertains the crowds gathered below for the naming ceremony of No.66723.*

Bottom Left: *This is surely one of the most impressive name plaques ever to be unveiled on a modern diesel locomotive. The plaque depicts a Chinook along with the crests of No.7, 18 and 27 Squadrons of the RAF, who are responsible for flying Chinook helicopters.*

Previously:

Page 107: *One of the highlights of the day takes place in the afternoon (luckily in between the rain showers!) with a staged event involving the newly named No.66723 and a Chinook helicopter.*

A run past takes place on the Kettering North Junction - Manton Junction line with the Chinook hovering above No.66723 as it passes over the famous Harringworth viaduct, a stunning result!

Dave Granger, RAF Shawbury

Above: *Class 66/7 No.66723 waits patiently in the mornng sunshine at First GBRf's Wellingborough yard for the official dignitaries to arrive and unveil the locomotive's new name plaque.*

Below: *It's smiles all round as First GBRf Managing Director, John Smith, presents a 'Chinook' plaque to Wing Commander Richard Mason (Left) and Station Commander Group Captain Andy Turner (Right) a truly great day and my thanks go to First GBRf for their kind invitation.* **Martin Buck (4)**

FOLKESTONE HARBOUR

'R.I.P.'

Or will there be a reprieve? Well, this is the question being asked (at the time) following the last train (a filming special) to leave Folkestone Harbour on 12th April - a light engine move involving three First GBRf Class 73 locomotives.

Earlier that day, Kingfisher Tours' 'Golden Arrow' steam charter (1Z29, 06:07 ex-Taunton) arrives at the harbour terminus behind Class 67 No.67006 *'Royal Sovereign'*, with un-rebuilt 'Battle of Britain' 4-6-2 No.34067 *'Tangmere'* on the rear of the train for the return journey; thus, 'Tangmere' has the distinction of possibly being the last steam locomotive to work the Folkestone Harbour branch.

The department of Transport, EWS and South Eastern are all objecting to the closure, the site earmarked for re-development into a marina.

Top Right: *A commemorative wreath carried by No.73204 'Janice' for the occasion.*   **Richard Jones**

Opposite: *A stunning photograph ....   Electro-diesels No. 73204 'Janice' + No.73205 'Jeanette' + No.73209 'Alison' are dwarfed by the cliffs as they pass Folkestone Warren, watched by two fans. The trio are running as 0Z73, the 14:45 Folkestone Harbour - Hoo Junction.*   **Nick Slocombe**

Below: *The electro-diesels explode detonators on the track causing seagulls to take flight as they cross the arches of the harbour viaduct at Folkestone.*   **Richard Jones**

'EDs' - Daylight Running

Above: *The movement of the remaining Class 73 Electro-Diesels is closely followed by enthusiasts living in the South East of England, especially if they operate during daylight hours. The driver of the leading 'ED' is clearly distracted by something by the lineside as Nos.73136 'Perseverance' + 73208 'Kirsten' pass Tudeley, near Tonbridge, on 5th July with 6G13, Canterbury East - Hither Green engineer's train.* **Alan Hazleden**

Below: *This is the second of a series of workings carrying demolition waste from the Brighton Lovers Walk shed to Eastleigh, the first of which takes place on 15th October, operated by top 'n' tail First GBRF Class 66s. However, the second working on 22nd October features the semi-permanent coupling of Nos.73208 'Kirsten' + 73206 'Lisa', which are seen crossing Farlington Viaduct with 6G30, the 12:15 Lovers Walk - Eastleigh.* **Nic Joynson**

'Blockade Busters'

Above: *Due to the expansion of WCML engineering works and the consequent disruption to weekend passengers, Virgin Trains introduce a Voyager service on Saturdays between Birmingham and London Euston, via the Chiltern route, with the co-operation of Chiltern, EWS and Network Rail. The service commences on 28th June, but on 17th August, complications in diagramming a Class 221 Voyager into London Euston results in Mk3 set WB64 being used on the service with DVT 82101 on the rear. Virgin Trains Class 57, No.57313 'Tracy Island' accelerates through Saunderton leading 1Z40, the 11:00 London Euston - Wolverhampton.* **James Welham**

Below: *Meanwhile, some four miles further north, No.57313 is seen again at Horsenden Lane on the approach to Princes Risborough with the 1Z40 service from Euston. The running lines between here and Saunderton diverge and the 'Up' main line runs through the 83-yard long Saunderton Tunnel.* **Dave Stracey**

Capital Stuff!

Tuesday, 26th August, is a day of diversions, caused by the on-going upgrade of the WCML which closes it at Rugby until 06:00hrs on Wednesday 27th. As a result, DRS, EWS and Freightliner are running their services over unusual routes and, as is often the way of these things, not everything down to run, actually runs. That makes for one of the joys of the rail enthusiast's hobby - unpredictability - busily wandering around London for much of the day, seemingly missing some things whilst copping others. And the weather, is at least dry (which for August is a plus!).

There then follows a period of more diversions due to engineering work, between Willesden and Gospel Oak. All trains which normally pass through the 'High Level' platforms, or use the 'Kensal Green Chord' are subject to diversion / retiming until mid-November for ten weeks, effective 1st September, resulting in all cross London traffic to be re-routed via Primrose Hill and Camden Road.

Above: *Anglo-Scottish DRS services between Grangemouth / Coatbridge and Daventry are being routed via the ECML and the North London Line, such as 4M30 headed by No.66430, seen on 26th August between Camden Road and Primrose Hill; shame all the containers were on the rear of the train!*

Top Left: *Not a freight diversion as such, but definitely a locomotive working 'off route' when Class 66/4 No.66411 'Eddie The Engine' makes the headlines away from its normal 'Tesco Express' duties. Here, 'Eddie' is double-heading 4M71, Tilbury - Daventry intermodal along with No.66417, running through Highbury & Islington station with a rake of empty container flats in tow.*

Bottom Left: *A consequence of these diversions is that Camden Road becomes even busier and is a good place to see both 'scheduled' and 'diverted' freight at close quarters. A colourful ensemble slowly approaches Camden Road with Freightliner's green-liveried Class 90 No.90041 hauling a rake of red Hamburg Sud containers; one service unaffected by the diversions, 4L41, Daventry - Felixstowe.* **Nick Slocombe (3)**

Below: *Four days later, engineering blockades on both the WCML and MML results in 6H50, Willesden - Tunstead cement empties taking a circuitous route home via Kensington Olympia, Kew, Willesden, Gospel Oak, Finsbury Park, Hertford Loop, the ECML and Sheffield. The train, headed by No.60040 'The Territorial Army Centenary', passes through Kensington Olympia hauling a lengthy rake of JGA bogie tank hoppers.* **Ralf Edge**

LOCOMOTIVE GALLERY

Carlisle 'Curios'

Above: *A train spotters bonanza - four locomotives at the head of a train instead of one!*

The 6K05, Carlisle Yard - Crewe Basford Hall departmental service is often used by EWS to reposition locos and on 24th July, No.66012 heads 6K05 through Carlsile Citadel, inclusive of Nos.66076, 66075 and 66116 DIT in the consist of railway sleepers.

Below: *New and old side by side.... as the smoke and steam billowing from Britannia Pacific No.70013 'Oliver Cromwell' begins to clear, Carlisle 'Thunderbird' No.57308 'Tin Tin' is revealed stabled in the carriage sidings awaiting the next turn of duty. 'Oliver Cromwell' is in the process of working Kingfisher's 'Dalesman' charter from Hellifield to Carlisle and back on 27th August.*   **Andrew Naylor (2)**

Colas 'Curios'

Above: *Nine Mk2 coaches superbly painted in blue & grey livery by Cargo-D are moved from Long Marston to Crewe by Colas Rail's No.47727 'Rebecca'on 25 September and the train (5Z47) is seen passing the well-tried vantage point of Lower Moor, near Pershore, on the Cotswold Line; 110$^{1}/_{2}$ miles from London Paddington.*

Below: *Eight days later, 3rd October, and 'Rebecca' is back out again on stock moves. Having taken eight Virgin liveried Mk2 coaches from Oxley to Long Marston as 5Z47 in the morning, No.47727 returns with four Freightliner HXA coal hoppers and deliver them to Stoke Gifford, near Bristol. The ensemble, headed by the brightly coloured Class 47 and running as 6Z47, Long Marston - Crewe, passes the site of Defford station on the Birmingham - Bristol main line, following a reversal at Worcester*   . **Peter Tandy (2)**

59s OFF THE BEATEN TRACK

Top Left: *On 20th May, Class 59/0 No.59004 'Paul A Hammond' awaits departure from the Calvert trans-shipment facility with 6Z48, Calvert - Acton Yard spoil empties; this reportedly being the only time a Mendip Rail Class 59 has been seen working this particular service.*
Dave Stracey

Middle: *Three months later and the very unusual sight of a Class 59 locomotive working the Midland Main Line on 15th August. No.59204 'Vale of Glamorgan' heads north with a rake of empty MEA 2-axle box wagons at Kibworth Harcourt, six-miles north of Market Harborough, running as 6Z56, the 13:41 Southall Yard - Healey Mills. The locomotive then ran light engine to Toton TMD for tyre turning.*
Andy Small

Bottom left: *Yet still further afield, in Germany, we see one of the original members of the five-strong Foster Yeoman Class 59/0 fleet.*

Now sporting Heavy Haul Power International branding, No.59003 'Yeoman Highlander' heads the 13:00 Berlin New Seddin Yard - Krakow ballast empties through Genshagener Heide (on the Berlin ring) on 24th September.

No.59003 was taken out of traffic at Merehead on 29th November 1996 and after many modifications was transferred to mainland Europe on 1st May 1996 in the consist of the 09:33 Dollands Moor - Lille 'Connectrail' service, thence onwards to Saarbrucken, Germany.

The reason for the move lies in Foster Yeoman's desire to expand its aggregate business in Europe, knowing that large quantities of aggregate would be needed in Germany. A link up with DB Cargo ensued and, as part of the deal, Foster Yeoman would supply a Class 59 locomotive, which culminated in the full repaint of No.59003 into a joint Yeoman / DB Cargo red / blue colour scheme.
Chris Perkins

Viva L'Espana!

Above: *After overhaul at Axiom Rail, Eastleigh, four ex-EWS Class 58s (Nos. 58015, 58021, 58047 and 58050) appear in Continental Rail blue and yellow, destined for work on a new high-speed line being constructed in Spain from Barcelona to Figueras. Two of these, Nos.58015 and 58047, are seen 'DIT' behind Class 66/0 No.66069, hauling 6M44, Eastleigh - Wembley 'Enterprise' at Clapham Junction, on the first leg of their journey. All four locomotives move through the Channel Tunnel on 18th September.* **Michael Wright**

WSMR DVTs

Below: *Friday, 10th October sees the first run of a Wrexham, Shropshire & Marylebone Railway DVT, No.82301, south of Crewe. The train is 1Z09, Crewe - Marylebone which is running about 50-minutes late passing Leamington Spa, propelled through the 'Up' main line by No.67015. The first revenue earning run of a WSMR DVT takes place the following day, on Saturday 11th October, using the same train set on the 1P03, 08:55hrs ex-Wrexham / 1J87, 15:17hrs ex-London Marylebone diagram.* **Peter Tandy**

INDUSTRIAL RELATIONS

Corus On View

Left: *The Appleby Frodingham Railway Preservation Society gala on 10th & 11th May, includes passenger trips around the Corus steelworks complex, Scunthorpe. Locomotives on view include ex-BR Class 20 No.20056, now numbered 81, which is seen at Gate E*

Below: *Meanwhile, remote controlled Yorkshire Engine Company 'Janus' 0-6-0 shunting locomotive is seen hauling steel bar at the Medium Section Mill. In the background, there is a rake of JTA / JUA tipplers, off the Immingham - Santon Gate iron ore circuit.*

Settle Speakman Pier Branch

Opposite: *The branch is located at Queenborough on the Isle of Sheppey (near Sheerness), operated by Istil (UK) and, despite the appalling condition of the track in some places, it is still in use. The steelworks at Queenborough receives steel ingots by ship, which is unloaded at a wharf about a mile away from the works onto ex-BR bogie wagons. The steel is then turned into various types of steel bar, reloaded onto the wagons, and taken to an unloading site. This view shows Andrew Barclay 0-6-0 shunting locomotive No.873 on the line leading to the wharf with two wagons loaded with steel bars.*

Richard Jones (3)

FREIGHTLINER TURNS

Perfect Symmetry

Above: *A brief visit to Ipswich on New Year's Day (2008) sees the stabling point playing host to two Freightliner Class 90 electric locomotives and three unidentified Class 66/5s awaiting their next turn of duty. In this perfectly balanced view, the two Class 90s display remnants of the former British Rail era where a cast metal 'Depot Plaque' and 'Double Arrows' once adorned the cabside of No.90043 and No.90049, respectively.* **James Welham**

Opposite: ### Stalwart 'Cans'

Top Left: *The early bird catches the worm, in this case 4L89, Coatbridge - Felixstowe freightliner around about 08:00hrs on the morning of 29th March. This service is 'booked' for Class 90 traction, but the cameraman is pleased to see a brace of Class 86s (Nos.86627 and 86612) sweeping round the curve at Old Linslade at the head of the train; the first 86s seen on this train for sometime.* **Nick Slocombe**

Bottom Left: *Class 86/6s normally work in pairs, but one freightliner is actually diagrammed for single Class 86 operation - 4L41, Daventry - Felixstowe (4M41 return) - viewed on 27th February behind No.86637, travelling along the 'Down' North London Line No.1 at Barnsbury Junction, approaching Caledonian Road & Barnsbury station. Note the direct current lines running alongside the North London AC lines.* **Nigel Gibbs**

Overleaf: ### Two's Company, but Three ....

Page 124 (Top Left): *Three corporate liveries for three Class 90s and a scene that will not be seen again! In the obligatory dull spell, Freightliner's Green liveried No.90016 leads 'One' liveried No.90015 and Freightliner Grey No.90047 DIT through Kelvedon on 14th November 2007 with 4M88, Felixstowe - Crewe.*

(Bottom Left): *On 25th April, Freightliner's Class 86s, Nos.86605 + 86639 double-head 4L89, the 22:00 Coatbridge - Felixstowe freightliner service, north through Marks Tey, which on this particular occasion includes No. 66591 in the consist, albeit not providing power.* **James Welham (2)**

Page 125 (Top Right): *Freightliner Class 66/5 No.66567 heads north with 4S59, Southampton - Coatbridge with two Class 57s (Nos.57004 and 57003) dead in tow and minus their nameplates. The train is approaching Wormleighton Crossing at 17:22hrs on the beautiful evening of Friday, 4th April. The Class 57s will be removed from the train at Crewe Basford Hall.* **Geoff Plumb**

(Bottom Right): *On 12th August, two Freightliner Class 86s, Nos.86614 and 86638, come to grief on the Great Eastern Mainline near Ilford when No.86614 develops a fault while working 4L89, the 22:00 Coatbridge - Felixstowe North. The train makes it as far as Brentwood on the 'Electric Lines' where it is declared a failure. National Express East Anglia's Class 90 No.90006 is the nearest available loco at Ilford EMUD which is promptly sent to assist the ailing train. Running as 0P99, No.90006 makes the short run to Shenfield, where it reverses for the short run back to Brentwood to drag the ensemble to Ipswich Yard. The trio are pictured passing Ingatestone at 12:22hrs, running nearly two hours behind schedule.* **James Welham**

FAREWELL 'ELECTRIC SCOTS'

The end of 2007 not only marks the end of a year, but also the end of an era, as the final curtain comes down on Class 87 operations on the main line. A Class 87 'Electric Scot Farewell' tour scheduled to run on 29th December 2007 between Birmingham International to Glasgow Central is cancelled at the last minute, much to the annoyance of passengers waiting at various pick-up points

Sadly, with the exception of the Class 87s detailed below, all the remaining members stored at Long Marston (as at 1st January 2008) will be exported to Bulgaria for planned use on freight traffic:

Number	Original Name	Status	Location
87001	Royal Scot	Preserved	York, National Rail Museum
87002	Royal Sovereign	Preserved	Long Marston
87005	City of London	Scrapped	
87012	Coeur de Lion	Active	Bulgaria
87015	Howard of Effingham	Scrapped	
87016	Sir Francis Drake	Scrapped	
87019	Sir Winston Churchill	Active	Bulgaria
87024	Lord of the Isles	Scrapped	
87031	Hal o' the Wynd	Preserved	Tyseley
87035	Robert Burns	Preserved	Crewe
87101	Stephenson	Scrapped	

However, on the plus side, the AC Electric Goup secure No. 87002 'Royal Sovereign' and since its arrival at Long Marston at the end of January 2008, the Group's main line team have undertaken a full E-exam, fitted OTMR equipment and completed a repaint from the previous Porterbrook livery back into BR Blue. The locomotive has been reunited with its old name 'Royal Sovereign'. It was originally named in 1978 and carried it until 2003 when it was repainted into purple livery to promote its then owners, Porterbrook Leasing. It remained nameless until April 2005 when it was named 'The AC Locomotive Group' at Wembley. It has the distinction of heading the last 'official' Virgin West Coast diagrammed Class 87-hauled train with No.87010 on 10th June 2005, and hauled the 'really' very last Virgin diagrammed Class 87-hauled train on 22nd December 2006.

Above: On 22nd April, Class 66/7 No.66723 tows three Class 87s (Nos.87026, 87008, 87007) to Crewe for testing before being shipped to Bulgaria. Running as 0M89, Long Marston - Crewe, the 66/7 is out of view running round, leaving the three 87s awaiting departure from Crewe station shortly before dusk. All three locomotives carry Bulgarian Railways branding and No.87026 sports an interesting combination of green and yellow. **Guy Houston**

West Coast Reminiscences

Above: *The author has fond memories of the Class 87 'Electric Scots', running in multiple on heavily laden Anglo-Scottish freightliners and Dee Marsh steel trains, not to mention the Euston - Glasgow passenger expresses. On 1st June 1980, No.87032 'Kenilworth' arrives at Carlisle with 1S57, the 10:45 London Euston - Glasgow Central 'Royal Scot' formed of a rake of Mk3 vehicles.*

Below: *Nos.87002 'Royal Sovereign' + 87035 'Robert Burns' double-head 6M24, the 05:40 Mossend - Dee Marsh steel on 10th August 1984, a service these electrics will work as far as Warrington, before handing over to diesel traction for the remainder of the journey.* **Martin Buck (2)**

LOCOMOTIVE GALLERY

Above: *Beautifully restored and turned out in original BR Blue livery, No.87002 'Royal Sovereign' poses for the cameras at Long Marston as part of the Class 87 Farewell event held on 7th June.*

Below: *Meanwhile, Nos.87028 'Lord President' and 87022 'Cock o' the North' stand inside the shed awaiting repair in readiness for export and a new life in Bulgaria.* **Richard Jones (2)**

87002's Main Line Return

Above: *The AC Electric Group's Class 87 No.87002 'Royal Sovereign' successfully hauls its first main line test run in preservation from Crewe to Carstairs and return on 16th July, with no major problems to report during the runs. The train includes No.86101 'Sir William A. Stanier FRS' as backup and a rake of five Cargo-D Mk3 vehicles. On the return journey, double-heading is dispensed with and No.87002 speeds south through Hest Bank with 1Z88, the 13:00 Carstairs - Crewe; a view reminiscent of the late 1970's / early 1980's.*

It is worth noting the considerable help needed to see a restoration project such as this through to a successful conclusion; LNWR for examinations and repair work at Crewe, TCL for the certification and inspection, Sharpe Engineering for the OTMR design and fitment, Brecknell Willis for pantograph overhaul and ETS for workshop facilities at Long Marston, not to mention the support of the AC Electric Group's members.

Below: *Back in action, albeit in typical 2008 weather, on 14th October, No.87002 passes Penrith with three Class 325 units in tow, which form 1M44, the 15:34 Shieldmuir - Warrington mail.* **Andrew Naylor (2)**

LOCOMOTIVE GALLERY

Extra Capacity

Above: *To provide more accommodation, especially during busy periods, Cross Country is returning five High Speed Trains to its routes, providing an extra 842 seats across the fleet. The first refurbished power cars are due to enter service in July, followed by the first complete set in September. Until then, XC are utilising Ex-Midland Mainline set XC04 to cover the diagram (9V57, 08:50 Edinburgh - Penzance and 9S66, 08:30 Penzance – Dundee) and on 8th June, 9V57 passes over Hayle viaduct nearing journey's end with Paxman Valenta engined No.43184 leading and No.43007 tailing the set. The diagram runs under a 'Class 9' headcode to alert signallers that such services cover long-distances and timeliness is essential to avoid delaying other services.* **James Welham**

Below: *Aberdeen, for the first time in almost 6 years, regains an HST operated Cross Country service with a set being diagrammed for the weekdays 9S53, 06:40 Plymouth - Aberdeen. In the beautiful autumnal light, we see No.43321 leading / No.43301 rear of the first run north (its second day in service) of Arriva's refurbished HST. On Tuesday, 30th September, 9S53 passes the golf links at Inverpeffer on the approach to Arbroath.* **Jim Ramsay**

200 for 7 in 50 YEARS

1958 - 2008

Background: 18th April 2008 marks the 50th anniversary of one of the most popular (in my case, <u>the</u> most popular!) class of diesel locomotive to ever grace Britain's railways. The Class 40s were the first Type 4 to be delivered as part of the 1955 Modernisation Plan and were employed on a mixture of passenger and freight duties. The first ten were used on Great Eastern expresses between London and Norwich (D200 - D204) and Nos. D205 - D209 on Great Northern turns like the *'Flying Scotsman'* and *'Master Cutler'*, before being displaced on the latter trains by Deltics and Peaks, respectively.

After the success of the prototypes, another 190 locomotives were ordered, numbered from D210 to D399. All were built at Vulcan Foundry, except a batch of twenty (Nos. D305 - D324) which were built at Robert Stephenson and Hawthorns factory in Darlington. All the locomotives were painted in British Railway's green livery and the final locomotive (No. D399) was delivered in September 1962.

Design: Batches of the class were built with significant design differences, due to changes in railway working practices. The first 125 locomotives (Nos. D200 - D324) were built with 'disc' headcode markers, which BR used to identify services. However, it was later decided that locomotives should display a four character train reporting number (headcode) and Nos. D324 - D344 were built with 'split' headcode boxes, which displayed two characters either side of the locomotive's central gangway doors. Gangway doors were eventually done away with and the remaining locomotives (Nos. D345 - D399) carried a central four-character headcode box. Seven of the first batch of locomotives, Nos. D260 -D266, were later converted to the central headcode design.

Names & Numbers: Nos. D210 - D235 were named after ocean liners operated by Cunard, Elder Dempster and Canadian Pacific, as they hauled express trains to Liverpool, the home port of these companies. The one exception being No. D226 which was to carry the name *'Media'* but never did so. From approximately 1970, with Class 40s no longer working these trains, the nameplates were sadly removed.

From 1973, locomotives were renumbered under TOPS and became known as Class 40s; locomotives D201 to D399 were renumbered in sequence, becoming 40001 to 40199. The first built, D200, was renumbered 40122, which was vacant due to the scrapping of D322 after an accident.

Above: *No.40122 numbered as D200 outside Grosmont shed, North Yorkshire Moors Railway.* **Carl Gorse**

Decline: The Class 40s operated in most areas of British Railways (except the Western and Southern Regions) and in the years leading up to withdrawal were based at depots in northern England, notably Gateshead, Healey Mills, Longsight, Kingmoor, Springs Branch, Thornaby and York.

In later life, the locomotives were mainly found hauling heavy freight and passenger trains in the north of England and Scotland and, due partly to their lack of electric train heating, they lost their last front-line passenger duties in Scotland in 1980; their last regular passenger duties being on the North Wales Coast Line.

By the end of 1984 only thirteen were still running, including pioneer locomotive No.40122 (D200), which was reprieved in July 1983 and painted in the original green livery to haul rail enthusiast's specials. The last passenger run by a Class 40 (No.40122 excluding) took place on 27th January 1985, when No.40012 hauled a train from Birmingham New Street to York. All the remaining locomotives (except No.40122) were withdrawn the next day.

Class 40 withdrawals began in 1976, when three locomotives (Nos.40005, 40039 and 40102) were taken out of service and, thereafter, further withdrawals were inevitable due to a combination of circumstances - a lack of air braking on some members, leaving them unable to haul more modern freight and passenger vehicles, and many developing bogie fractures. Nos.40012, 40060, 400118 and 40135 were briefly reinstated in 1985 for departmental duties connected with the Crewe station remodelling and signalling scheme and numbered 97407, 97405, 97408 and 97406, respectively.

Into Preservation: Fortunately, seven Class 40s were saved from the cutters torch, although this is a comparatively meagre number, when compared to other locomotive classes. They are:

Number	Initial TMD	Intro.	With.	Owner	Home Base
40012	Willesden	06.59	04.86	Class 40 Appeal	Midland Railway Centre, Butterley
40013	Willesden	06.59	01.85	Private Owner	Barrow Hill Roundhouse
40106	Crewe North	11.60	04.83	Private Owner	Nene Valley Railway, Peterborough
40118	Crewe North	02.61	09.85	D318 Ltd	Birmingham Railway Museum, Tyseley
40122	Norwich	03.58	04.88	National Collection	National Rail Museum, York
40135	Crewe North	03.61	01.85	CFPS	East Lancs Railway, Bury
40145	Neville Hill	05.61	06.83	CFPS	East Lancs Railway, Bury

However, seven it is, and in the next few pages I have included a selection of pre and post-preservation images, plus a further three images to record a personal tribute to the Class.

40013

Top Right: *The fourth 'namer' in the series, No.40013 'Andania', arrived at Barrow Hill on 14th January 2003 and, after engine repairs, was successfully restarted on 8th June 2003; moving under her own power for the first time in preservation on Sunday, 15th June 2003.*

This view shows No.40013 in the process of being repainted at Barrow Hill, prior to receiving green livery. **Richard Jones**

Bottom Left: *On 25th July 1980, No.40013, minus her 'Andania' nameplates, slows for the Abergele station stop with 1D11, the 11:18 Crewe - Holyhead.* **Martin Buck**

40118

Middle: *This particular 'whistler' (so called because of the distinctive turbocharger noise) was built by Robert Stephenson and Hawthorn, Darlington, and last of the RHS batch to be withdrawn, outliving No.40124 by more than 2 years. She is seen here languishing at Tyseley with major restoration work still to be carried out.* **John Binch**

Below: *On 1st June 1980, No.40118 awaits the road at Preston on a light engine move to Blackburn to take up ballast duties.* **Martin Buck**

D200 (40122)

Above: *On New Year's Day, 1981, No.40122 is seen at Guide Bridge, Greater Manchester; the stabling point for diesels which interchange with Class 76 'Tommy' electric locomotives working the now-closed Woodhead Route.*

Below: *Pioneer D200 is currently based at the North Yorkshire Moors Railway. Following withdrawal in August 1981, the loco was restored as part of an apprentice training scheme at Toton TMD, receiving the power unit from No.40076 in the process, returning to traffic in April 1983. D200 is seen at Dent on 31st July 1983 during a photo-stop, while in charge of 1Z12, the 08:48 King's Cross - Carlisle 'Hadrian Pullman'.* **Martin Buck (2)**

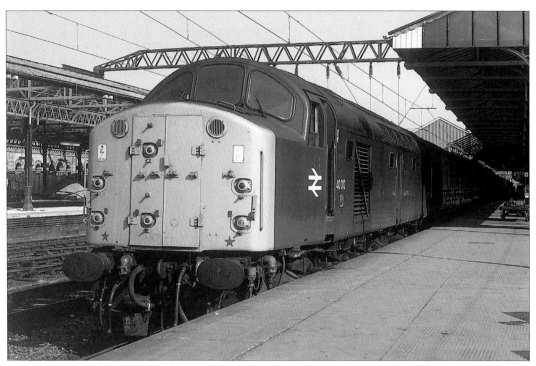

40012

Above: *Weekend engineering work between Preston and Crewe would result in passenger services being diverted and diesel-hauled off the electrified route via Manchester or Chester, often with the main train engine (an AC Electric locomotive) being 'dragged' DIT as well. On 2nd August 1981, No.40012 has arrived at Crewe with 1A10, the 07:05 Blackpool North - London Euston, having been diverted via Manchester Oxford Road.* **Martin Buck**

Below: *No.40012 poses for the camera at Swanwick, Midland Railway Centre, on 16th February, looking resplendent after overhaul as D212 in Brunswick-Green livery and complete with 'Aureol' nameplates.* **Carl Gorse**

Left: *On 11th August 1984, No.40106, now renumbered D306, is named 'Atlantic Conveyor' in memory of the Cunard cargo ship and those on board who lost their lives in the 1982 Falklands war.*

The name was dedicated by John Brocklehurst, Chief Officer of the ship, although some of the Class 40 purists did not agree with this naming as the locomotive never carried a name during her working life. **Andrew Naylor**

40106

Page 136: *No.40106 was one of 20 Class 40s (Nos. 40105 to 40124) built at the Robert Stephenson and Hawthorn factory in Darlington, allowing production capacity at Vulcan Foundry to build the 22 'Deltics'. After years of anonymous hard work with the rest of the fleet, by 1978 the loco was among a handful of Class 40s which hadn't been repainted into BR Blue and yellow. During her last works overhaul at Crewe in September 1978, the loco was repainted into blue and yellow, but shortly afterwards it was decided to repaint the loco in Brunswick Green with full yellow ends. Prior to this, No.40106 is seen on the fuelling point at Inverness TMD on 11th April 1976 in readiness to work a passenger express south over the Highland Line.* **Martin Buck**

Page 137: *In April 1983, No.40106 was withdrawn from BR traffic, deemed 'life expired' and less useful having only vacuum train brakes. It was subsequently bought by Gerald Boden in March 1984 and delivered to the Great Central Railway on 18th April 1984, which happened to be the 26th anniversary of D200's inaugural working from London Liverpool Street. The locomotive is always in pristine condition, as we see in this view of her runnning as D306 on 26th April during the Nene Valley Railway's 1960's weekend, passing Ailsworth with the 14:18 Orton Mere - Wansford 'goods'.* **Nigel Gibbs**

40135

Below: *After a spell running as No.97406 for the Crewe remodelling scheme, withdrawal from British Rail service finally came on 16th December 1986. Along with No.40012, split-box No.40135 was put on the BR tender list and, following lengthy negotiations, she was secured by the Class Forty Preservation Society (CFPS) in May 1988, and delivered to Bury later that year. The locomotive's home base is still Bury on the East Lancashire Railway, where she has been painstakingly restored to full working order and painted in green livery. No.40135, operating under the pre-TOPS number of D335 is seen at Bury Bolton Street.* **Richard Jones**

Above: *On New Year's Eve 1979, when there were more sociable things to do, a weekend visit to the North West of England was a good time to see plenty of 'whistlers' on shed. This is Northwich, prior to the local church bells heralding in the new year, and No.40135 stabled outside the old steam shed.*

Below: *No.40135 entered service on 11th March 1961 and was allocated to no less than eight depots in a working life spanning 24 years, staying at Longsight TMD from May 1975 until withdrawal in January 1985. On 23rd July 1982, the driver gets a bit of shut eye in the cab of No.40135 before departing from Bangor with empty vans bound for Red Bank carriage sidings, Manchester.* **Martin Buck (2)**

40145

Below: *D345 was the first locomotive of the final delivery batches, fitted with centre-headcode panels, entering service on 17th May 1961 and one of four (D345 to D348) to be allocated to 55H Neville Hill for use on the 'Queen of Scots Pullman' running between Leeds and Edinburgh / Glasgow, replacing L.N.E.R. Pacifics. She was based at Longsight until withdrawal on 10th June 1983 after sustaining derailment damage in Stourton Yard, Leeds, and was purchased by the CFPS and delivered to Bury in February 1984, the first Class 40 to enter preservation. On 7th June 1980, No.40145 is seen heading through Chester station with a well loaded Willesden - Holyhead freightliner; the Class 40 taking over from electric traction at Crewe, Basford Hall.*　　　　**Martin Buck**

Previously:

Page 140:

Top Left: *No.40145 gained a certificate for mainline operation on 28th October 2002 and hauled her first mainline railtour since preservation the same year, on 30th November 2002 - 'The Christmas Cracker IV'. On 25th July 2007, No.40145 is named 'East Lancashire Railway' at Bury and is repainted in BR Blue Large Logo livery complete with 'wrap-round' yellow front ends, sponsored by DVD producers Visions International, as a result of a poll of CFPS members. I have pleasure in offering a selection of four images depicting No.40145 at work in her present guise as a tribute to her enduring performance and pleasure she brings to so many enthusiasts. The first image shows No.40145 on 15th September 2007 (No.37248 DIT on rear) passing Edale with 1Z45, the 12:00 Buxton - Heysham leg of the 'Buxton Forester'.*　　　　**Nigel Gibbs**

Bottom Left: *One week earlier, in the South West of England, a superb view of No.40145 powering over the summit at Whiteball with 1Z55, the 06:39 'Devonian' charter runing from Banbury to Kingswear.*　　**Chris Perkins**

Page 141:

Top Right: *Perhaps, 'Working of the Year'! On 9th May, the 'whistler' finds herself working 6Z40, the 14:00 York - Heywood taking a Network Rail Water Cannon to the East Lancashire Railway for testing and is seen passing through Paddock cutting, near Huddersfield. This was to be the second time in less than a month for No.40145 to work a freight train. On 15th April, Class 60 No.60030 in charge of 6M61, Humber - Bedworth, was wrongly routed at Nuneaton Abbey Junction towards Hinckley. The nearest locomotive happened to be No.40145, which was summoned to drag the train back onto the WCML.*　　　　**Neil Harvey**

Bottom Right: *OK, so the sun does not always shine when you want it to, but this is England, and photographs of the Copy Pit route between Hall Royd Junction and Burnley seldom feature. On 14th June, looking towards a patchwork of green fields, No.40145 thrashes it's way up to Copy Pit Summit (749ft. above sea level) with 1Z07, the 16:48 Manchester Victoria - Blackburn 'Cotton Mill Express'.*　　　　**Neil Harvey**

Personal Recollections

While travelling back from a stint working on the narrow guage Welshpool & Llanfair Light Railway in the summer of 1972, as my DMU entered Shrewsbury, I was greeted by a sight that would ultimately shape my interest in railways for years to come. Stabled at the station were two green-liveried diesel locomotives, the likes of which I had never seen before having grown up in the diesel hydraulic mecca of Swindon with a staple diet of Warships, Westerns and Hymeks.

I soon discovered they were Class 40s, the longest diesel on BR at 69ft. 6ins. in length with two eight-wheel bogies carrying a frame which housed an English Electric engine providing 2,000 horse power, lumbering giants nicknamed 'Big Ds', 'Buckets' and 'Whistlers'. I decided there and then to try and scratch off every one of the 200-strong fleet in my Ian Allan spotting book; a task which took until 10th December 1975 when the last one to see, No.40182, was recorded at Guide Bridge, just in time before it left on a rake of empty bogie tanks bound for the British Oxygen plant at Widnes.

My interest then switched to photography, with all but nine examples of the Class recorded on slide film for posterity, the highlight seeing them hard at work on unfitted freight trains climbing to Ais Gill Summit; two such images are reproduced overleaf.

Hindsight is a wonderful thing and I only wish I started my 'haulage years' earlier. By the time I did so in 1980, many 'vacuum brake-only' members started to be withdrawn and I would have probably chalked up a journey behind more than 147 members of the Class, had I done so. That said, travelling behind Class 40s was something I would not have missed and having amassed a meagre 50,000 miles of haulage, memories there are a plenty - too many to list, but two readily spring to mind, both involving No.40168. The first occasion being on 18th April 1981 and a 310-mile out & back trip from Glasgow Queen Street to Aberdeen (probably my favourite journey of all) followed on the 21st July 1984 when 1,000 miles of BR scheduled service train mileage was chalked up behind '168 leaving Leeds with 1M26 bound for Carlisle.

Of course, it all had to end somewhere, but I could hardly imagine the end of the journey for so many Class 40s would actually be here in Swindon, destined for scrap in a diesel hydraulic graveyard!

Above: *Having been withdrawn from active service on 1st December 1980, Carlisle Kingmoor based No.40105 languishes in Swindon Works yard on 17th February 1981, where the process of dismantling is well underway.*

Overleaf:

Page 144: *Having successfully tackled 15-miles of a ruling 1 in 100 gradient from Ormside, the driver of No.40176 eases off the power as 7A09, the 11:31 Carlisle - Willesden breasts Ais Gill summit (1,169 ft. above sea level) and prepares to descend all the way to Settle Junction. Looking back, you can see how severe the final part of the climb is and the magnificent sight of Wild Boar Fell providing the backdrop.*

Page 145: *With just under 2-miles to go to reach Ais Gill, ex-works No.40009 passes Lunds on 4th June 1980 hauling a short rake of loaded 2-axle 'Presflo' cement tanks from Clitheroe to Hexham. The northern portal of Moorcock Tunnel is visible in the background.* **Martin Buck (3)**

OPEN to the PUBLIC

The Summer of 2008 sees several depots and works open their doors to the public, including Carnforth, Crewe Gresty Bridge, Heaton, Hope cement works, Knottingley TMD and Merehead; too many to feature in these pages, but a small selection is included for the record.

DRS, Gresty Bridge, Crewe

Direct Rail Services (DRS) hold an open day at its Gresty Bridge depot on 19th July, which officially opened on the 23rd March 2007 with the blessing of the late Hon. Mrs Gwyneth Dunwoody MP. The new depot was part of DRS's business expansion programme providing maintenance facilities to allow the company to have its its own maintenance works. It also opened up opportunities for DRS to have a better control of the quality, timetabling and scheduling for maintenance, as well as providing a valuable maintenance capability for use by other train operating companies.

The Open day raises funds for DRS's charitable causes and, as with last year's Kingmoor Open Day, entry is restricted to ticket access only.

Left: *DRS 'Choppers' No.20313 + No.20310 stand inside the shed with No.66411 'Eddie the Engine' visible at the end of this line.*

Below: *Ex-Freightliner Class 57 No.57002, minus 'Freightliner Phoenix' nameplates and still in green livery, is stabled on the same line as 'Police' Class 47/8 No.47829 and DRS Class 37/6 No.37609.*

Top Right: *On the day, Class 47/4 No.47501 is named 'Craftsman' and is stabled alongside recently re-liveried sister locomotive No.47832 'Solway Princess. The black cloth used to mask the nameplate prior to the unveiling can still be seen attached to the locomotive.*

Heaton 'Community' Day

For over 130 years, the people of Heaton and its surroundings have helped to keep the railways running and Newcastle's Heaton T&RSMD hosts an open day on 14th September. TOC Northern invite the public to join them at Heaton and to celebrate its railway heritage and its place within the community. They can see how trains are maintained, displays of how the depot used to be and plans for the future, along with local community stalls and classic steam & diesel locomotive exhibits.

Above: *This illustration shows off the main protagonists of East Coast Main Line passenger operations dating back to before the outbreak of the Second World war. From left to right, the locomotives on display at Heaton are NXEC Class 91 power car No.91111, 4-6-2 Pacific No.60007 'Sir Nigel Gresley', Class 55 Deltic No.55022 'Royal Scots Grey' and Great Central HST power car No.43068, partially visible. Perhaps, while the young lad enjoys his chips, let's hope he enjoyed the day sufficiently to come back for more!* **Carl Gorse (4)**

LOCOMOTIVE GALLERY

Cranmore '150'

To commemorate 150 years since the opening of the East Somerset Railway between Witham and Shepton Mallet in 1858, the East Somerset Railway and MendipRail at nearby Merehead hold a gala to celebrate the railways in Mendip, with several visiting locos. attending.

As part of the event, five pairs of shuttle trains run on 21st and 22nd June between Westbury and Cranmore in top 'n' tail formation. Train engines are EWS Class 66/0 No.66200 on both days and Mendip Rail Class 59 Nos.59001 *Yeoman Endeavour* and 59102 *'Village of Chantry'* on the 21st and 22nd, respectively.

Above: *Several main line locomotives are on display at Merehead during the weekend, such as in this view taken on Saturday, 21st June, where the line up is (from left to right) Nos.66623, 59102, 66731, 59104, 59103, 59203, 60040, plus No.59002 in the small shed in the background.* **Robert Sherwood**

Opposite: *Inside the main shed at Merehead, sheltered from any bad weather, sales stalls are assembled, hoping to attract the wallets of passing enthusiasts. Looking out into the yard, Class 59/1 No.59104 'Village of Great Elm' is stabled alongside GBRf Class 66/7 No.66731.* **James Welham**

Below: *Mendip Rail Class 59/0 No.59001 'Yeoman Endeavour' tails 1Z16, the 15:30 Westbury - Cranmore away from Westbury station on 21st June; the leading engine is Class 66/0 No.66200, out of view.* **Jamie Doig**

LOCOMOTIVE GALLERY

Carnforth 1968 - 2008

It is fitting Carnforth should hold an open day weekend in 2008 (26th & 27th July) as, 40 years ago in August 1968, we said farewell to steam on British Rail and Carnforth MPD (10A), along with Rose Grove MPD (10F) and Lostock Hall MPD (10D), which were the last operational steam sheds in the country. Today, Carnforth remains in active use as headquarters of WCRC and, due to the amount of shunting and train preparation on the site, it's 11 years since the public were last here.

Above: *The WCRC fleet comprises a staggering 111 locomotives (not all operational) with 4 steam, 39 Class 33 & 37 and 68 Class 47 & 57 locomotives and here is a classic line up of a small selection stabled in the sidings: from left to right, No.37668, 37165, 37717, 37517, 47489, 47526, 47772, 47492 and 47525.*

Below: *'Compass' liveried Class 37/0 No.37229 'Jonty Jarvis' heads a row of DRS traction on display, stabled alongside two Carnforth landmarks - the mechanical coal and ash disposal plants - the ash plant is the only one of its kind in existence in the UK and the concrete coaling plant only one of two in existence.* **Michael Wright (2)**

Hope Cement Works

'Old & New'

Right:

Lafarge complete a major rail infrastructure upgrade at its Hope cement works, which will see it move a large proportion of its cement distribution on to rail and achieve a reduction in lorry loads of 6,800 each year.

On 4th September, 'Blue Circle' branded shunting locomotive No.773 'Blue John' brings some PCA 2-Axle cement tanks into the newly commissioned yard and passes some of the new JPA bogie cement wagons used on the West Thurrock flow. This unique diesel hydraulic locomotive was delivered by the Scottish firm of Hunslet Barclay in 1989.

Below:

New house colours for Lafarge are displayed on HNRC's Class 20 No.20168 'Sir George Earle' following overhaul at Barrow Hill - a smart looking white livery with green solebar and cab.

Ralf Edge (2)

SILVERLINK 'SWANSONG'

To mark the end of the Silverlink franchise in November 2007, Pathfinder Tours organise two tours for 3rd and 10th November, covering most of the lines in Silverlink's network, as well as a few bits of rare track. The second tour runs on the last day before the franchise is split up between new operators, London Overground and London Midland.

Traction for both tours will operate in top 'n' tail mode, involving the following locomotives:

> 3rd.   No. 37410 *'Aluminium 100'* + No. 37417 *'Richard Trevithick'*
>
> 10th.   No. 37410 *'Aluminium 100'* + No. 50049 *'Defiance'*
>
> Stock : 5350 + 5040 + 4927 + 5009 + 1863 + 3112 + 3107 + 21272

An added bonus is the provision of Silverlink's Class 08 No. 08874 'Catherine', which will haul each train from Bletchley TMD to Bletchley station.

The two tour details are as follows:

3rd.	10th.		
1Z33	1Z46	08:21,	London Euston - Tring
1Z34	1Z47	10:14,	Tring - Barking
1Z35	1Z48	12:16,	Barking - Bletchley TMD
1Z36	1Z49	15:50,	Bletchley TMD - Northampton Kings Heath
1Z37	1Z50	19:49,	Northampton Kings Heath - London Euston

The departure times shown above are those scheduled for the 3rd November tour, with only minor timing alterations for the second tour.

Above: *Running on the direct current lines, the Silverlink Swansong 1 charter passes Bushey with No.37410 at the rear of the train, sixteen miles into the first leg of the day's itinerary. Meanwhile, Class 58 EMU No.508301 is about to depart with 2C14, the 09:21 Watford Junction - London Euston.*   **Nigel Gibbs (3)**

Above: *Another 'rear end view', but this time with No.37417 featured as the train passes Willesden Junction on 3rd November with No.37410 heading away from the camera with 1Z34, the 10:14 Tring - Barking.*

Below: *Silverlink Swansong Mk.2 and the third leg of the charter, 1Z40, the 12:16 Barking - Bletchley TMD. Class 50 No.50049 has come off the Tottenham & Hampstead Line and now waits at Gospel Oak for the signal to follow a Stratford - Richmond passenger working onto the North London Line and some more interesting destinations, including Bletchley TMD and Flyover, Swanbourne Siding and Northampton Kings Heath EMU depot.*

LINDUM FAYRE

The annual Lincoln Christmas Fayre attracts a large number of visitors from across the country with railtours over three days of festivities (7th / 8th / 9th December 2007) operating from London, Nottingham, Salisbury, Southend and Scotland. Traction for the railtours is quite diverse, providing photographers with the opportunity to shoot a variety of heritage locomotive classes in the Lincolnshire countryside, sadly though in less than favourable weather conditions as it turns out! Here's a small selection of the special trains running on 7th December 2007.

1Z82, London Victoria - Lincoln VSOE

Top Left: *After No.67029 arrives at Lincoln with the 1Z82, VSOE luxury dining special from London Victoria, the ECS (5Z82) with No.67005 'Queen's Messenger'on the rear, leaves Lincoln bound for stablling at Barnetby. Note the semaphore signal, which disappears in August under the Lincoln resignalling programme.* **Guy Houston**

1Z18, Linlithgow - Lincoln

Middle: *The SRPS charter from Linlithgow approaches Saxilby on the Doncaster to Lincoln line and the combined enjoyment of Deltic haulage in the shape of No.55022 'Royal Scots Grey' and shopping, more than makes up for the 05:40hrs start time for the passengers on board.* **Alan Hazelden**

1T61, Nottingham - Lincoln 'Shuttle'

Bottom Left: *West Coast Railway Company Class 47/8 No.47804 and No.47787 at the rear, pass through Collingham on the Nottingham - Lincoln main line with the outward leg of a 'shuttle' laid on by East Midlands Trains to ferry people to and from Lincoln Market. During the three days, the weather is not good for photography, dark, cold and windy on the Friday and Saturday is 10 times worse - very, very, very wet!* **Mick Tindall**

'SPIN & WIN'

1Z12, Wembley EFOC - London Euston   'Moor & More'

Above: *On 15th December 2007, Pathfinder Tours operate one of their 'Spin and Win' style rail tours from Gloucester to Dollands Moor, aimed at the traction enthusiast market and featuring a number of different locomotive changes during the day. The 'Moor and More' is no exception and includes haulage at different times by a veritable feast of freight locomotives: Nos.66703, 66170, 73205 & 73209, 90016, 66158, and 92029. With such a large number of changes, timekeeping can be problematical, but the tour is largely trouble free. Having taken over the train at Wembley Yard, No.92029 'Dante' is seen approaching Kemsing, broadly on time with 1Z12 heading for Dollands Moor and a change of traction for the run to Euston.* **Alan Hazelden**

STOBART PULLMAN

Luxury all the way ....

Stobart Rail and Direct Rail Services (DRS) launch their new joint venture on 12th February with a luncheon special from London to Fareham. On board, 200 invited guests enjoy at-seat hospitality from Premier Train Catering in Mk.3 carriages. The train departs from London Victoria's Platform 2 at 10:43hrs travelling a non-stop "Wessex Circular" route via Basingstoke, Andover and Fareham, returning via Haslemere and Guildford to London Euston at 16:09hrs.

The Stobart Pullman has been created as a result of a merger between Eddie Stobart and Westbury Group, which includes Victa Westlink Rail and Hertfordshire Railtours. DRS provide the traction for the Stobart Group and their charter business has been overhauled and relaunched as a luxury dining experience. The launch train comprises two immaculate Class 47/7 locomotives - Nos.47712 *Pride of Carlisle* and 47802 *Pride of Cumbria* - and a Mk.3 formation, plus two Mk.1 restaurant cars and a Mk.2 brake vehicle, numbers:

11030 / 80042 / 11019 / 11044 / 11046 / 1657 / 11054 / 11013 / 17159

Victa Westlink postscript

Victa Westlink Rail, a company formed from the remnants of FM Rail, has been closed down by its new owners, Eddie Stobart Group, having lasted less than 300 days and reportedly making a loss of £3m - £4m in the period. Highlights included the launch of an intermodal service between Ditton / Grangemouth and Purfleet using hired-in DRS Class 66/4s and a rake of KAA Mega 3 'Pocket' wagons, plus the appearance of Class 47/8 No.47832 in Victa Westlink colours.

Short lived ....

However, the Stobart Group decides to end its Pullman luxury charter operations in July because it is deemed 'not part of the core business', although rumours suggest that low bookings may have played a part in the decision. The last train visited the West Highlands of Scotland between 4th - 7th July.

Above: *Patiently waiting for the off, recently repainted Class 47/8 No.47832 heads the 'Stobart Pullman' at London's King's Cross station platform 2 on 15th June, with 1Z47, the 11:30 Father's Day special to Norwich. Class 47/7 No.47712 is on the rear of the train out of view.* **Nigel Gibbs**

Above: *In rather eye-catching corporate livery, the inaugural tour (1Z88, Victoria - Fareham) is pictured passing a foggy Wandsworth Road on 12th February, hauled by newly named and repainted No.47712 'Pride of Carlisle'; No.47802 'Pride of Cumbria' is DIT on the rear.* **Alan Hazelden**

Overleaf :

Page 158: *The quintessential 'chocolate box' view of Knaresborough Viaduct, built in 1851 and spanning the River Nidd. In this view, No.47802 'Pride of Cumbria' brings up the rear of 1Z47, the 08:18 King's Cross - Harrogate (headed by No.47712 'Pride of Carlisle') on 26th April; the train being the 'Harrogate Spring Flower Show' Stobart Pullman.* **Neil Harvey**

Page 159: *The scourge of the plastic bag .... if ever graphic evidence were needed to highlight the problem, then look no further than this excellent illustration of No.47712 leading 1Z60, the 07:25 King's Cross - Carlisle on the outward leg of the tour via the Tyne Valley Line at Gateshead Metro Centre on 23rd February.* **Carl Gorse**

Below: *On this particular occasion, No.47501 heads the Stobart Express (1Z47 06:52 ex-Paddinton) to Shrewsbury via Swindon and Hereford past Cattybrook at the western end of Patchway tunnel on 28th February 2008. Note, the lines here are at different levels, running through separate tunnel bores.* **Chris Perkins**

SPITFIRE RAILTOURS

Spitfire Railtours is a family run company dedicated to providing value for money railtours for the discerning rail traveller, committed to using classic British heritage locomotives on a range of routes which reflect their former 'glory days'.

Unfortunately, their first attempts to run a train in 2007 end in failure, when the inaugural charter from London King's Cross to Edinburgh has to be postponed and later cancellled due to the 'Deltic' undergoing power unit repairs. Furthemore, their sell-out 'Class 87 Farewell' charter also has to be cancelled on the day due to problems with the coaching stock.

Undeterred, Spitfire Railtours persevere and run their first train on 23rd February taking No. 55022 'Royal Scots Grey' across the Pennines and onto the ECML from Liverpool Lime Street to Edinburgh Waverley. Future railtours are planned with DRS Class 20s and Class 37s, plus others.

1Z55, Liverpool Lime Street - Edinburgh Waverley   *'Deltic Pioneer'*

Above: *Reminiscent of former glories, No.55022 'Royal Scots Grey' departs from Newcastle with Spitfire Railtour's inaugural charter, 1Z55, the 06:14 Liverpool Lime Street - Edinburgh on 23rd February. I suspect the organisers were slightly worried when the stock did not arrive on time from Carnforth and the charter subsequently departs from Liverpool 40 minutes late!*   **Carl Gorse**

1Z70, Birmingham International - Carlisle   *'Cumbrian Explorer'*

Top Right: *An immaculate pair of DRS Class 37s, No.37667 + No.37688 'Kingmoor TMD' are turned out on 8th March to work 1Z70, the 07:16 Birmingham International - Carlisle 'Cumbrian Explorer'. The train is seen passing Carnforth having actually departed from Birmingham New Street at 08:35hrs as the 'booked' start point of Birmingham International is scuppered as all signals in the area were out due to cable theft.*   **Andrew Naylor**

1Z30, Crewe - Weymouth   *'Wey-Farer'*

Bottom Right: *Another Spitfire tour and another choice of motive power. On an extremely dull & dreary 19th April, Class 20s No.20310 + No.20307 accelerate away from Eastleigh heading for the South Coast. Class 57 No. 57601 is on the rear of the train for ETH purposes only.*   **James Welham**

'BUFFER - PUFFER 6.0'

The 'Buffer-Puffer' concept is very popular and comprises a number of mini-tours (seven, in this case!), visiting a selection of Southern Region London termini and branches. This particular one features top 'n' tail Class 37s working the Riviera Trains 'British Classic' train set of refurbished traditional Mk.1 First and Standard class 'Chocolate and Cream' coaches, which represent the classic BR Western Region livery carried in the late 1950s and early 1960s.

While very enjoyable for enthusiasts, this type of tour is a logistical nightmare for the operating authorities and due to extreme pathing issues encountered with the original routing, a revised routing is adopted. To give readers a flavour of its complexity, the route is reproduced below:

Itinerary:

(1Z37): London Bridge - Metropolitan Jn - Charing Cross - Metropolitan Jn - Cannon Street - Metropolitan Jn - Blackfriars - Loughborough Jn - Herne Hill - Tulse Hill - Balham - Clapham Junction - Kensington Olympia - Willesden West London Jn - Acton Wells Jn - South Acton Jn - Old Kew Jn - Hounslow - Twickenham - Barnes - Clapham Junction - Ludgate GW Jn - Factory Jn - Brixton - Herne Hill - Tulse Hill - Streatham - Selhurst - East Croydon - Oxted - Uckfield

(1Z38): Uckfield - Oxted - East Croydon - East Grinstead

(1Z39): East Grinstead - Oxted - Norwood Junction - Crystal Palace - Tulse Hill - Peckham Rye - London Bridge

(1Z40): London Bridge - Peckham Rye - Denmark Hill - Factory Jn - Stewarts Lane Jn - Victoria

(1Z41): Victoria - Battersea Park - Factory Jn - Peckham Rye - Nunhead - Lewisham - Eltham - Falconwood - Slade Green - Charlton - Lewisham Vale Jn - Tanners Hill Jn - North Kent East Jn - London Bridge - Cannon Street

(1Z42): Cannon Street - Metropolitan Jn - Blackfriars - Loughborough Jn - Canterbury Road Jn - Factory Jn - Latchmere Jn - Kensington Olympia - Willesden Junction HL - Gospel Oak - South Tottenham East Jn - Tottenham South Jn - Copper Mill Jn - Temple Mills East Jn - High Meads Jn - Lea Jn - Dalston Kingsland - Canonbury West Jn - Finsbury Park - Alexandra Palace - Gordon Hill (Bay Platform)

(1Z43): Gordon Hill - Bowes Park - Via Up Goods Lines - Finsbury Park - London King's Cross

Above: *On 2nd February, No.37401 is seen crossing the lattice structure of Oxted Viaduct, with the third leg of 'Buffer-Puffer 6', the 1Z39, the 15:19 East Grinstead - London Bridge. The viaduct spans the A25 road, which is now not so busy due to the adjacent M25 motorway.* **Nigel Gibbs**

1Z37, Crewe - London Fenchurch Street *'The Grays Church Elegy'*

Above: *Finally, having reached the Network Rail limit at Thames Haven, No.37417 has run around and, along with No.37401, the pair now double-head the last leg of the charter, 1Z39, the 16:13 Thames Haven - Crewe, running around 20 minutes behind schedule. The duo storm past the 'Classic' shot on the Thames Haven branch with the refinery in the background heading towards Thames Haven Junction, where it will join the London, Tilbury & Southend line before making the long journey north to Crewe.*

Below: *Earlier, on 26th April, having run round at Temple Mills, No.37401 now leads 1Z37 towards Limehouse and the destination of the first leg, London Fenchurch Street. The C2C Class 357 alongside the charter was held whilst the charter crossed over from Bow Junction. Locos over this stretch are extremely sparse with only a handful of test trains and charters annually.* **James Welham (2)**

Saturday, 9th February, marks the date of the second railtour to run under the UK Railtours banner (*a priori* Hertfordshire Railtours), the first being the 'Preston Docker' on 19th January 2008.

The tour departs from London Victoria and travels around the South London Suburbs, ending up at Alton and the Mid Hants Railway. The return journey is through some of the South West Suburbs before heading in to London Waterloo via the Shepcote Lane chord.

'OOZLUM BIRD No. 2'

1Z96, London Victoria - Alresford

Top Right: *Journey's end and a well-deserved rest for the two 'Electric Bluebirds as they pose for the cameramen at London Waterloo station, having brought the return charter (1Z97) back to the Capital.* **Carl Gorse**

Top Left: *Traction for the 'Oozlum Bird 2' will be 2 x GBRF Class 73s, No.73209 'Alison' + No.73206 'Lisa', and whatever the Mid Hants Railway can provide. On the outward journey, the two 'EDs' pass Haydons Road on the Streatham Junction - Wimbledon line with 1Z96, 08:55 ex-Victoria. Note, the Oozlum bird, also spelled Ouzelum, is a legendary creature found in Australian and British folk tales & legends; some versions have it that, when startled, the bird will take off and fly around in ever-decreasing circles until it manages to fly up itself, disappearing completely, which adds to its rarity!* **Iain Scotchman**

Bottom Left: *Having already taken a circuitous route from Victoria: Tulse Hil - Mitcham Junction - Sutton Junction - Wimbledon - Brixton, 1Z96 is seen again some two hours and 32 miles later passing through Norwood Junction, heading for Alton via Redhill, Guildford and Aldershot.* **Nigel Gibbs**

Below: *At Alton MHR Passing Loop, Class 33 No.6593 (TOPS No.33208) is attached to the rear of 1Z96 for the 10-mile run along the Mid Hants railway to Alresford and is seen upon arrival. The 'Slim Jim', sporting Brunswick green livery with yellow front warning panel, then couples up to the two EDs + coaches for the run back down to Alton, from where the tour engines take over for the homeward run.* **Carl Gorse**

STIRLING - ALLOA - KINCARDINE
Official Opening

The official opening of the new line from Stirling to Alloa and Kincardine (SAK) takes place on 15th May with a shuttle service of special trains operating between Stirling and Alloa to mark the occasion. The line was originally due to open in the summer of 2007 and it is not until 2nd April 2008 when First ScotRail begin driver training between Stirling and Alloa using a Class 158 unit. Three days later, the first coal train uses the line when No.66083 hauls 6G18, the 13:00 Hunterston - Longannet, formed of EWS loaded HTA bogie hoppers. The opening of the new line will see coal trains running direct to Longannet without the need of going via the Forth Bridge and a reversal at Thornton yards.

Above: *On 15th May, No.55022 'Royal Scots Grey' hauls one of the special 'shuttles' past Causewayhead, Stirling, onto the newly laid track of the SAK, leaving a trail of distinctive 'blue' exhaust in her wake. The train is 1Z97, the 16:30 Stirling - Alloa, which has K4 2-6-0 steam locomotive No.61994 'The Great Marquess' on the rear to work the return journey, 1Z98, 17:30 Alloa - Stirling. The River Forth runs alongside the track at this point and the vantage point is Abbey Craig, at the top of which stands The National Wallace Monument.* **Jim Ramsay**

TYNESIDE 'COMBOS'

1Z70, Manchester Victoria - Newcastle   *'Tynesider'*

Top Right: *Leaving Manchester at 06:37hrs on 2nd February, 4-6-2 Pacific No.71000 'Duke of Gloucester' is in sparkling form, both externally and in terms of its performance as she heads across the Pennines and down the ECML to Newcastle. Unfortunately, the train is brought to a standstill on the 'Up and Down' slow line south of Low Fell Junction as the front of the locomotive passes a signal at danger (SPAD). The driver is relieved of driving the train, with Network Rail insisting that No.71000 and its train be hauled into Newcastle by a diesel locomotive. With the Castle Keep in the background, No.66048 heads 1Z70 into Newcastle Central.*

1Z54, London King's Cross - Newcastle   *'Choppington Changer'*

Bottom Right: *Variety of motive power is a sure way to attract passengers onto a railtour, such as the 'Choppington Chopper' on 15th March, featuring locomotive classes 56, 60, 66 and 92 during the day. No.92022 'Charles Dickens' leads 1Z55 away from King's Cross before handing over to No.56303 for the run to Newcastle. Here, DRS No.66423 is coupled to the front of the train and this close up view shows the duo leaving Newcastle with 1Z55, the 14:43 to Doncaster.* **Carl Gorse (2)**

86259 *'Les Ross'*

When Class 86/2 No.86259 first arrived at Tyseley, it was devoid of nameplates, following a period in store. It has since been repainted into BR Electric Blue livery and, on 8th February, the loco completed its main line test run successfully and became a main line registered locomotive.

This 25kV AC electric locomotive was built at Doncaster in 1966 and entered service with the number E3137. It was renumbered into the TOPS scheme as No.86045 and was later rebuilt as an '86/2', becoming No.86259.

It received the name 'Peter Pan' in 1979 when BR recommenced naming locomotives. However, it was renamed in 1995 to 'Greater Manchester The Life & Soul Of Britain'. In 2002 it was further renamed by Virgin Trains to 'Les Ross' a Birmingham based DJ. The locomotive was a regular performer on the Birmingham New Street to London Euston trains at that time, until withdrawal from service in October 2003.

1Z86, Birmingham New Street - Preston *'Les Ross's Day Tripper'*

Top Left: *The first railtour for the second AC Electric locomotive to be privately restored to main line service - Les Ross's No.86259 - runs on 1st March, in two parts: Birmingham New Street to Liverpool Lime Street in the morning (and returning in the afternoon); plus, in between, a triangular "turning trip" via Preston and Crewe. A credit to the team at Tyseley, No.86259 looks to have been beautifully restored as she stands upon arrival at Liverpool Lime Street's platform 6, having arrived three minutes late with 1Z86, the 08:30 Birmingham New Street - Preston.*

Middle: *Silver BR Lion and Wheel cast metal emblem on the bodyside of No. 86259.* **Mark Riley (2)**

Bottom Left: *Some two hours after leaving Liverpool, No.86259 passes Balshaw Lane on the return 1Z87, 13:14 Preston - Birmingham New Street with No.47773 DIT on the rear. The 47 works the 'triangular move' in order for No.86259 to be facing south for the departure from Liverpool back to Birmingham later in the afternoon. The Class 47 actually worked two legs of the tour: Liverpool Lime Street - Rainhill - Earlestown - Wigan North Western - Preston followed by Crewe - Runcorn - Liverpool Lime Street.* **Fred Kerr**

1Z14, Whitby - Perth *'Esk Valley Scotsman'*

Above: *On Saturday, 8th March, WCRC Class 47s No.47787 and 47826 top 'n' tail the 'Railtourer' 1Z14, 07:30 Whitby - Perth charter, which No.47787 leads to Perth following a mandatory reversal at Battersby. On the return journey, No.47826 awaits departure time at Perth with 1Z15, the 15:38hrs to Whitby.* **Carl Gorse**

Western Champion

Breaking (More) New Ground!

In 2007, Class 52 diesel-hydraulic No. D1015 'Western Champion' breaks new ground by working a charter train over Cambrian metals to Aberystwyth for the first time. Whilst some people do not advocate diesel locomotives working to areas of the country or over lines unrepresentative of their days in active BR service, I think in this case an exception can be made.

There can be little doubt that the 'Westerns' (or 'Thousands', as they were also affectionately known) are iconic and will continue to grace any stage on which they happen to perform, looking completely at home in unfamiliar surroundings.

'Western Champion' could equally run under the name 'Western Pioneer' as she makes even more forays into previously unchartered territory. Highlights include an outing along the North Wales Coast line to Holyhead, a charter run in conjunction with Pathfinder Tours and the Irish Traction Group. The ITG is unable to run tours in Eire at the present time due to an Irish Rail ban on the majority of charters while it awaits for commissioning of new Korean DMUs to be completed.

There then follows a challenging sortie to the Scottish Capital, Edinburgh, where there are many highlights along the way. For example, a run along the Tyne Valley, crossing the Royal Border Bridge at Berwick-upon-Tweed for a first visit of the Class North of the Border, plus a southbound ascent of famous Beattock Bank! A selection of images of these two ground-breaking charters follow:

1Z15, Ealing Broadway - Holyhead   *'Irish Mail'*

Above: *On 16th February, No.1015 accelerates away from Holyhead on the return leg of the journey, 1Z51, the 15:15 Holyhead - Ealing Broadway, a round trip of 344 route miles. A total of 74 of these diesel-hydraulic locomotives were built between 1961 - 1964 and operated on the Western Region of British Railways. Containing two Maybach MD655 diesel engines coupled to Voith hydraulic transmissions, these stylish-looking locos produce a massive 2700hp. Although given the designation "Class 52", these locos were never allocated TOPS numbers and were withdrawn during the 1970s.* **Mark Riley**

1Z52, Tame Bridge Parkway - Edinburgh   *'Western Scot'*

Above: *A majestic sight, if ever there was one! Sitting proudly high above the River Tweed, No.1015 crosses the Royal Border Bridge with 1Z52 and just about 4-miles to go before reaching the Anglo-Scottish border at Marshall Meadows.*   **Justin Buckley**

 Page 172: *With pocket camera ready in hand, a young lady gazes in awe at the spectacular sight of No.D1015 arriving 'under the wires' at Preston with 1Z52, the 05:10 Tame Bridge Parway - Edinburgh 'Western Scot' on 3rd May; passengers on board no doubt eagerly awaiting the ascent of Grayrigg and Shap!*   **Andrew Naylor**

 Page 173: *Just eight miles north of Beattock Summit (1,016ft above sea level) No.D1015 eases her 13 coaches through Abington Loops with the return 1Z53, 16:26 Edinbugh - Tame Bridge Parkway.*   **Guy Houston**

Below: *In the Edinburgh suburbs, with Edinburgh Castle dominating the skyline, No.1015 starts out on the 339-mile journey home passing Saughton with 1Z53, the 16:26 ex-Edinburgh 'Western Scot' and 13 vehicles in tow. Looking back, the junction is visible, which gives access to / from the Forth Rail Bridge.*   **Fred Kerr**

GOING DUTCH
Mercia Charters Limited
'All Good Things'
'Blaze of Glory'

The weekend of 21st and 22nd June, sees Mercia Charters organise two charters across the Channel in Holland, featuring ACTS Class 58 haulage, once a familiar sight on the East Midlands MGR coal circuit. It is, perhaps, a fitting moment to feature the Class, as EWS have mooted the possibility of Euro Cargo Ltd reactivating redundant Class 58s for use in Spain along with Class 56s in Poland, reguaging the former to run on 5ft 6in track. Of course, EWS already has eight Class 58s in Spain and a further three Class 58s (Nos. 58038 / 58039 / 58044) are in use in Holland with ACTS.

Locos : ACTS 5811 / 1254

Stock : 51 80 03 40 129-7 / 51 80 02 40 161-1 / 51 80 02 40 158-7 / 51 80 02 40 155-3

Train Details :

21st June

38000 : Rotterdam CS - Amersfoort
38001 : Amersfoort - Amersfoort Pon (Leusden)
38002 : Amersfoort Pon (Leusden) - Amersfoort
38003 : Amersfoort - Arnhem
38004 : Arnhem - Maastricht
38005 : Maastricht - Heerlen
38006 : Heerlen - Rotterdam CS

22nd June

38000 : Rotterdam CS - Amsterdam
38001 : Amsterdam - Sloehaven*
38002 : Sloehaven - Rotterdam

* Train diverted to Vlissingen as the freight branch to Sloehaven is closed for engineering work.

Above: *On the first day of the weekend programme, 21st June, No.5811 stands at Amersfoort Pon on the rear of the train, whilst Volker Rail locomotive No.203-1 'Tom' works the Amersfoort - Amersfoort Pon - Amersfoort leg of the 'All Good Things' tour.*

Top Right: *On the following day, No.5811 (ex-58039) and electric locomotive No.1254 are seen passing through Middleburg with the second Mercia railtour - 'Blaze of Glory' - heading for Vlissingen.*

Bottom Right: *You just can't get away from them .... Class 66 No.DE64 (PB06), operated by HGK, is observed running light engine through Utrecht Central on Saturday, 21st June.*   **Richard Jones (3)**

1Z33, Crewe - Weymouth   **'Great Wey Round'**

Above: *Having a soft spot for Class 33s, the photographer makes his way to the Bristol - Birmingham main line on a sunny, Saturday, 23rd August, to record a pair of WCRC-liveried examples working the 'Great Wey Round'. Nos.33207 'Jim Martin' + 33025 'Glen Falloch' approach Ashchurch with 1Z33, Crewe - Weymouth, where the narrower body of No.33207 is easily seen, as is the crew member in the cab of No.33025. It is presumed he is operating the ETH controls, if those in No.33207 are not working correctly.*   **Peter Tandy**

Below*: Meanwhile, the two 'Cromptons' are seen later in the day, again on the outward journey, climbing up to Bincombe tunnel, ten minutes out of Weymouth.*   **Nic Joynson**

5Z67, York - Old Oak Common

GBRf Special

Above: *After working a GBRF company train from York to York via Sunderland (1Z67), the ECS returns to base and in the early evening, 20:15hrs to be precise, 'Barbie' liveried Class 66/7 Nos.66731 + 66732 pass Sandy on 2nd July, heading 5Z67, the 17:38 York - Old Oak Common. These two locomotives, along with Nos.66728 - 66730, arrived at Newport Docks from EMD, Canada, in the hold of MV 'Jumbo Spirit' in April.* **Nigel Gibbs**

5Z68, Tees Yard - York

VSOE

Below: *On a gloomy, 10th September, the prestigious VSOE Pullman train is seen in Tees Yard amongst an assortment of steel carrying wagons and MGRs, about to depart behind Class 67s No.67021 + No.67001 with ECS forming 5Z68, Tees Yard - York, the carriages appearing quite unglamorous in such surroundings! The train had previously worked 1Z67, London King's Cross - York, then 5Z67 to Tees Yard to run the locos round and water the stock. This is a rare sight as ECS workings normally go to Tyne Yard and the coaches were (apparently) last reported in the North East in the early 1980s.* **Carl Gorse**

1Z45, Wolverhampton - Cleethorpes   *'Meridian Mariner'*

Above: *A rake of debranded Stobart Rail vehicles form the train set for Spitfire Railtours 'Meridian Mariner' from Wolverhampton to Cleethropes on 16th August, which is seen at Barnetby with No.37059 working solo atop No.37423 (DIT) + stock and No.47712 at the rear.*   **Carl Gorse**

1Z40, Bo'Ness - Ayr   *'Routes and Branches'*

Below: *On 24th August, the SRPS run the 'Routes and Branches' tour of the Strathclyde rail network using Class 40 No.40145 & Class 55 'Deltic' No.55022 in top 'n' tail formation from Bo'Ness to Ayr and back. The tour includes a visit to Glasgow Queen Street, Helensburgh Central, Ardrossan Harbour, Larkhall, Glasgow Central Low Level and Springburn. On arrival at Queen Street, No.55022 shuts down, resulting in it being hauled 'Dead in train' on the rear back to Bo'Ness. In this view, No.40145 brings 1Z55, Ayr - Bo'Ness back down the Larkhall branch and passes through Chatelherault station for the 2nd time at 17:57hrs.*   **Guy Houston**

Above: *Towards the end of the 2007 RHTT season, DRS Class 37s No.37261 and No.37194 top 'n' tail the Crewe - Holyhead RHTT, approaching Abergele on 15th November 2007. In fact, the train is almost a secondary feature to the semaphore signals dominating the view in the foreground.* **Fred Kerr**

The Granite City Beckons

Below: *When a Class 37 locomotive appears North of the Border, Scottish-based rail photographers still regard such occurrences as too good to miss, as this small selection illustrates. A regular sight on the Aberdeen route is pipes from Hartlepool bound for Laurencekirk, conveyed on 6A30, Mossend - Aberdeen 'Enterprise.' The train is 'booked' a 'shed' but, on 1st December 2007, attracts EWS Class 37/4 No.37405 and is seen passing Larbert on time at 11:08hrs, whilst on her way for winter snow duties in Aberdeen.* **Guy Houston**

Bottom: *No.37422 'Cardiff Canton' with Class 67 No.67009 DIT heads north through Carnoustie on 9th January with the 04:40 Edinburgh - Aberdeen portion of the Caledonian Sleeper. It is running over 6hrs late due to the train striking a fallen tree between Ladybank and Cupar. The 37 came on at Dundee after the Tay Rail Bridge re-opens after the winds subside.* **Jim Ramsay**

Above: *On 28th December 2007, No.37422 'Cardiff Canton' idles at Aberdeen station awaiting departure time with 0A31, Mossend - Aberdeen Waterloo Goods, formed of empty ICA china clay tanks fom Irvine, Ayrshire.*

Below: *Then, in rapidly fading light, No.37422 does her best to obscure the view as she explodes into action, 'clagging' away form Aberdeen on the short trip (just over three miles) to the Croxton & Garry plant at Waterloo Goods. No.37422 was named 'Cardiff Canton' at Cardiff Canton TMD in March 2003.* **Jim Ramsay (2)**

One potato, two potato ....

Above: : *Shortly after being released from store at the end of the RHTT season, No.37515 collides with a lorry carrying potatoes at Whitemoss level crossing, between Gleneagles and Perth. This was during a light engine run from Grangemouth to Inverness for snowplough duties. The damaged 37 is seen in Blackford loop on 8th January with Class 66/4 No.66427, awaiting an overnight passage to Carlisle Kingmoor.* **Guy Houston**

Below: *On 18th February, No.37422 'Cardiff Canton' is diagrammed to work 6A67, Elgin - Laurencekirk and is seen here propelling its train of six IZAs into the 'Down Goods Loop' opposite Laurencekirk signalbox. Later in the day, Class 66/0 No.66001 arrives from Mossend to work the next leg of the journey, this being the daily (FX) 'Enterprise' service - 6D83, 16:08 Laurencekirk - Mossend.*

The loaded IZAs contain bagged seed potato, destined for East Anglia and cultivation into oven chips. After an overnight run to Doncaster, the loaded IZAs are then 'tripped' to Eccles Road, just over nine miles to the west of Wymondham on the Ely - Norwich main line. The seed potato is unloaded at the Snetterton railhead of Richard Johnston Ltd., which lies at the end of a short branch from Eccles Road. **Jim Ramsay**

'Bin' there, done it!

Right: *Occasionally, in 2008, the Edinburgh 'Binliner' can still produce a '37' if one just happens to be in the Millerhill area.*

A very overcast 21st March just happens to be a case in point.... EWS No.37405 approaches Prestonpans with 6B44, Oxwellmains - Powderhall with a a rake of rusting and shabby looking containers.

Guy Houston

A 'turn' for the worse

Above: *It's all down hill for No.37055 in 2008. Having been allocated in January to the WNSO pool (EWS Locomotives Sold, Awating Collection), she is removed from Thornaby on 9th February to Heanor's at Langley Mill, thence by road to EMR Kingsbury where she is cut up on 12th April. Prior to the move, beady eyes keep a watching brief over the 'tractor' whilst stabled in Thornaby depot yard.* **Carl Gorse**

Overleaf: **6F66 / 6F67 'Enterprise'**

Page 184: *News travels quickly when a 37 is about, with photographers making speedy positioning moves to secure that elusive shot and what better place to be, the Peak District. On 30th October 2007, Large Logo No.37425 'Pride of the Valleys' is paired with Brunswick Green No.37411 'Caerphilly Castle', seen high above the ground crossing Duke's Drive Viaduct, near Buxton, with 6F67, Dowlow - Warrington Arpley 'Enterprise', comprising covered Lime hoppers.* **John Rudd**

Page 185: *On 5th February, an immaculate No.37401 rounds the curve at Heathfield Nook, Harpur Hill, with 6F66, Warrington - Dowlow 'Enterprise' formed of empty Lime 'Covhops' from Mossend. One of the advantages of these two train services is that they travel at relatively slow speed due to gradients and a reversal in Buxton Yard in both directions, thus giving the opportunity to take photographs at several locations along the route.* **Ian Ball**

Warrington 'Trips':

Warrington is an ideal place for a Class 37 to find itself, as there are plenty of 'Enterprise' feeders and trips on which to find work. Destinations include:

- Blackburn   - Dallam
- Ditton   - Dowlow
- Gladstone Dock - Mostyn Dock
- Runcorn   - Sinfin
- Stanton Grove

As well as the two previous illustrations, here are three more 'trips.'

Top Left: *On one particular morning in February, No.37411 'Caerphilly Castle' passes through Warrington Bank Quay (Platform 3) with a rake of Cargowaggons, running as 6N42, Arpley - Blackburn.*

Middle: *The 8T15, Arpley - Dallam chemical tanks is usually worked by a Class 08 shunting locomotive. However, on 14th June, No.37401 has the trip, which comprises two Chlorodifluoromethane ICB Bogie tank wagons. The train is heading along the 'Up' Goods line at Bank Quay on the way to Dallam Freight teminal, a journey of just over 1-mile or so in length!* **Richard Spray (2)**

Below: *On 6th July, 'trip' 6N42 is seen again, but this time approaching Leyland station with No.37422 'Cardiff Canton' in charge.*
Fred Kerr

97301's First Time Out

Above: *Following overhaul at HNRC, Barrow Hill, No.97301 - formerly Class 37/0 No 37100 - is called into action on 23rd April to rescue a DBSO test run, which fails at Leicester. The train is 5Z47, the 05:45 Derby RTC - Derby RTC and is seen passing Wilmorton, Derby, with No.31601 bringing up the rear. This is the first EVER train to be worked by No.37901 since being exported to France in 1999.* **Ralf Edge**

Pointing the Way

Below: *Freshly embellished in 'Compass' livery, DRS No.37610 speeds south along the ECML at Sandy on 12th February with 6Z42, the 09:15 Doncaster Marshgate - Ashford stoneblower move. The locomotive is subsequently named on 17th April, 'T.S. (Ted) Cassidy 14.5.61-6.4.08', at Quorn on the Great Central.* **Nigel Gibbs**

1Q14

Above: *The moves of this particular working are closely followed by photographers, affording the opportunity to view DRS traction 'off the beaten track', such as on 7th May, when No.37038 brings up the rear of 1Q14 and No.37059 heads away from Highbury & Islington station towards Canonbury.* **Nick Slocombe**

Below: *On 6th February, No.37059 (No.37608 rear) skirts Hampstead Heath as it approaches Gospel Oak with 1Q14, the 09:31 Ilford - Cambridge via the North London line and Richmond.* **Nigel Gibbs**

Above: *On 5th July, the train makes a visit to the Sheerness branch with DRS Class 37s No.37259 and No.37612 providing the traction in top 'n' tail formation. In this view, 1Q14, Hither Green - Hither Green is approaching Queenborough with the Isle of Grain Power Station dominating the view in the background.*

Below: *Taking a photograph through a pane of glass is never easy, but this one seems to work pretty well. Seen from an elevated vantage point, in less than favourable light, No.37612 heads out of London Blackfriars with 1Q14, the 09:01 Selhurst - Selhurst on its way to Cannon Street on 10th July.* **Richard Jones (2)**

37401 Long Marston bound

Above: *The first batch of new bogie cement tanks from Germany arrives in the UK during February and, as a number of the wagons are not immediately allocated for operational use, they are moved for storage at Long Marston. On 19th March, 18 of the new Lafarge wagons (JPAs) leave Bescot Yard and Class 37/4 No.37401 is allocated for the move, which is seen approaching Stoke Works Junction en route to Worcester and the Cotswold line.* **Don Gatehouse**

Below: *Having taken the JPAs to Long Marston, No.37401 is rostered to return to Bescot with a rake of seven vans and the ensemble, which includes two Ferrywaggons, pass Pershore on the Cotswold Line.* **Peter Tandy**

37417 'Richard Trevithick'

Above: *The 'Little North Western' Route runs for just 34 chains shy of 25-miles from Carnforth to Settle Junction. Although it receives little photograhic attention, there are some pleasant vistas to be gleaned, like this one, which shows No.37417 'Richard Trevithick' crossing the River Luno at Arkholme on 30th April.* **Andrew Naylor**

Below: *On 5th June, No.37417 is summoned to move a rake of 30 spoil wagons from Warrington Arpley to Llandudno Junction (dropping half of them off at Ellesmere Port yard en route), running under a 6L30 headcode. The train is passing Upton-by-Chester on the Chester to Birkenhead line and as loco-hauled trains are now like the proverbial "hen's teeth", (even RHTTs are MPVs) it is good to see one - the Class 37 adds to the novelty!* **Geoff Morris**

4Z44, Haverton Hill - Carlisle Kingmoor

Above: *This working, along with the outward trip, can produce a variety of DRS traction. On a glorious Spring day in early March, a pair of Class 37s, No.37688 + No.37667, are rostered to work 4Z44, the 13:07 (WO) Haverton Hill - Carlisle Kingmoor returning wagons 'off repair' and the duo are seen passing Tees-Side Airport.* **Ian Ball**

Inspection Calls for 37423

Below: *After a lengthy overhaul at Brush, No.37423 is handed over to DRS in November 2007 and is initially put to work in March hauling the Network Rail inspection saloon No.999506 around the country. Looking resplendent, No.37423 has just been given the road at Middlesbrough, while on its first revenue-earning outing on 12th March; 2Z37, York - Whitby Network Rail special, as part of an investigation looking into the possibility of the North Yorkshire Moors Railway operating the Esk Valley route.* **Carl Gorse**

6X36, Didcot - Ashchurch

Above: *Ashchurch MOD sees regular trains from Didcot but, on 1st February, EWS hire No.37611 for 6X36, offering the unprecendented sight of a DRS locomotive hauling a single van and eight flats loaded with personnel carriers. The train, having run to Worcester Yard for the locomotive to run-round the wagons, is running past the exchange sidings at Ashchurch before reversing into the sidings and onto the branch, which once led to Redditch and on to Birmingham via Alvechurch and Barnt Green.* **Peter Tandy**

In Miniature

Below: *Well, not quite, but you could be forgiven in thinking this is a section of a model railway layout. It is, in fact, Gravesend station and DRS Class 37/4 No.37423 travelling along the 'Down North Kent' line on 6th August with Inspection Saloon No.975025 'Caroline' in tow, running as 2Z03, the 13:21 London Bridge - Grain.* **Richard Jones**

Two trains in one!

Above: *The Arriva liveried coaches stored at Long Marston finally move on 22nd September and DRS Class 37s No.37602 and No.37611 are given the job. Two trains (5Z74 and 5Z75) are scheduled to go to Eastleigh, but are interestingly coupled together at Long Marston for operational convenience and the short journey to Honeybourne, where the two trains will split. The odd looking combination of No.37602 and 5Z74 + No.37611 and 5Z75 are seen on arrival at Honeybourne.* **Peter Tandy**

37401 'In Town'

Below: *EWS No.37401 arrives in London from the South Coast on 26th August with 6M44, Eastleigh - Wembley 'Enterprise'. The loco is seen slowly entering Clapham Junction with a consist of four TEA Calcium Carbonate bogie tanks (ex-Quidhampton) and MoD containers (ex-Marchwood).* **Michael Wright**

Three for the price of One!

Above: *A DRS triple header, comprising Nos.37059, 37423 and 47712, works 4Z75, the 12:00 Wembley - Chaddesden Yard on 12th August. It is passing Pride Parkway, Wilmorton, (Derby) hauling 12 new IIA bogie coal hoppers for use on Fastline's burgeoning Ratcliffe power station coal flow.*

Overleaf: *Ex-EPS liveried locos. No.37603 and No.37601 join up with No.37667 for 2007 RHTT duties in East Anglia and all three are travelling back to their home base at the end of the season on 17th December 2007 crossing Beggars Bridge, Turves, with 6Z06 and four Water Cannon sets in tow.* **John Rudd**

Page 197: *No less than three Network Rail Class 97s are in the consist of 5Z97, the 05:45 Derby RTC - Derby RTC (via Sheffield, twice), which are seen passing Milford on 11th August with Nos.97301 and 97303 leading, plus No.97304 on the rear of the train.*

Below: *On 22nd September, we witness the unusual combination of DRS Class 37/4 No.37423 leading two Fastline 'Grids' No.56301 and No.56302 east through Spondon, running as 0Z41, the 10:30 Derby FMR - Brush Loughborough - some three hours late by all accounts!* **Ralf Edge (3)**

BR Blue - Large Logo

Above: *For many enthusiasts, the most popular choice of livery worn by a Class 37 locomotive is BR Blue-Large Logo, and these two images illustrate why. The first shows No.37314 'Dalzell' in sparkling 'ex-works' condition, passing Woodthorpe on the Great Central Line on 13th April with 1A28, the 14:10 Loughborough - Leicester North. No.37314 was re-numbered from No.37190 and named 'Dalzell' on 25th July 1986 at Motherwell TMD, reverting to No.37190 on 4th October 1988, and allocated to the FMGM 'Freight Metals Motherwell Pool'. Following brief spells at Thornaby and Cardiff, No.37314 was eventually withdrawn in 1993.* **Nigel Gibbs**

Below: *Class 37/0 No.37025 'Inverness TMD' looks truly impressive storming up the bank towards Birkhill on 29th December 2007 with 2S06, Bo'Ness - Birkhill during a 'Class 37 Running Day' on the Bo'Ness & Kinneil Railway. The combination of No.37025 and full winter sun is just too good an opportunity to miss!* **Guy Houston**

YEAR of the RAT

This title looks specifically at events in 2008 and, according to the Chinese Zodiac, 2008 is the Year of the Rat (Earth), beginning on 7th February and ending on 25th January 2009, the first in a cycle of 12 Animal signs, which recur every twelfth year. The Chinese celebrate with a bonanza of fireworks and festivals, but I will celebrate by reproducing three excellent 'Rat' images!

The Class 25s were built between 1963 and 1965 by British Rail Engineering Limited at Derby Locomotive Works and Beyer Peacock at Gorton, Greater Manchester - a total of 327. They were primarily designed for freight work, but some were fitted with boilers for heating passenger trains and throughout the 1970s they could be found nationwide, although the Southern Region never had an allocation. They were regular performers into the early 1980s on Crewe – Cardiff passenger trains and are fondly remembered for their use on summer-dated (Saturday) trains to Aberystwyth and Pwllheli, a task they relinquished in 1984. The final Class 25 loco. was withdrawn from service in March 1987.

The Class were ultimately divided into sub-classes:

Sub-Class	Original Numbers	TOPS Numbers	Type			
Class 25/0	D5151 - D5175	25001 - 25025	vo			
Class 25/1	D5176 - D5232	25026 - 25082	vb	vo	xb	xo
Class 25/2	D5233 - D5299	25083 - 25149	vb	vo	xb	xo
	D7500 - D7597	25150 - 25247	vb	vo	xb	xo
Class 25/3	D7598 - D7677	25248 - 25327	vo	xo		

Notes: vb = vacuum brake only, boiler fitted   vo = vacuum brake only, boiler isolated
        xb = dual brake, boiler fitted   xo = dual brake, boiler isolated

Above: *Here on the North Norfolk Railway, Class 25/0 No.25027 passes a non-functional fixed somersault distant signal adjacent to Sheringham golf course with a local service on 6th April. This locomotive received its BR Blue livery in 2007 and its last recorded passenger working in BR service is believed to be some 25 years ago on 18th March 1983 - 1J22, the 13:49 Bangor - Manchester Victoria.* **Nick Slocombe**

'STAR' ATTRACTION'

Below: *One of the star attractions at the Nene Valley Railway's Spring Diesel Gala on St. David's Day, 1st March, is First Capital Connect Hornsey depot pilot Class 03 No.03179 'Clive', seen on the turntable at Wansford. These quaint little locomotives (British Rail Class 03), along with Class 04, were one of BR's most successful 0-6-0 diesel-mechanical shunters, totalling 230 examples, built at BREL Swindon and Doncaster works during 1957 - 1962. They were numbered D2000 - D2199 and D2370 - D2399 and, following the withdrawal of the first four, became Nos. 03004 - 03399 and nicknamed 'Coffee Pots' by enthusiasts!* **Richard Jones**

A 'SWIFT' REPAINT!

Top Right: *Looking resplendent in BR Blue livery, Class 47/0 No.47270 poses for the cameras at Wansford following repaint and overhaul, which includes refitted bufferbeam cowlings and reinstated four-character headcode blinds. The 'Duff' was originally numbered No.1971 when built in 1965 and received the unofficial name 'Swift' at Tinsley TMD in 1990.* **Mick Tindall**

ADVENZA FIRST

Bottom Right: *Away from normal mainline duties, Advenza Freight Class 47/3 No.47375 visits the South Devon Railway for their Spring Gala held on 27th April. Flanked by two imposing examples of GWR lower quadrant semaphore signals, No.47375 arrives at Bishops Bridge loop with a freight working.* **Robert Sherwood**

Previously:

Page 200: *On the beautiful Llangollen Railway, resident Class 25 No.25313 puts in an appearance during a 3-day gala and is seen during one of the few sunny spells, running alongside the River Dee, approaching Glynyfrdwy on 12th April with the 13:50 Carrog - Llangollen. The 'Rat' is a surprise and, judging by its poor external condition, is in urgent need of an overhaul and repaint!* **Mark Riley**

Page 201: *The 'ice cream van' is back! As a result of a suggestion by members of the East Midlands Railway Photographic Society (EMRPS), No.D7677 (Class 25/3 No.25322 'Tamworth Castle') is returned to its 1984 'ice cream van' livery, complete with stencilled nameplate and bogie embellishments. The loco is seen at Cheddleton on the Churnet Valley Railway on 14th April during an EMPRS sponsored charter.* **Mick Tindall**

'BO - BO' GOLDEN JUBILEES

Part One: The 24 Quartet

The Class 24 was an early success from the 1955 British Rail Modernisation Plan and is still to this day proving to be a versatile design in railway preservation, although no surviving member runs on the main line. These Type 2s, numbered D5000 - D5150, were built in batches between 1958 and 1960 at Crewe, Darlington and Derby, with the first 20 (Nos.D5000 - D5019) built as prototypes fitted with a Sulzer 6LDA28A diesel engine.

The first 50 locomotives were classed as '24/0' and the final 101 locomotives were modified with smaller fuel tanks, the removal of an 'exciter' above the generator, so these examples were classified '24/1'. The last order, built at Derby in 1960, saw the greatest change in design with the installation of route indicators above the cabs. Furthermore, several (Nos.D5114 - D5132) were also fitted with recessed cab sides to cater for tablet-exchange for working on the Highland Main Line, Kyle and Far North lines. These locomotives were allocated to Inverness TMD and were also fitted with two headlights on the cab fronts.

When TOPS was introduced, the Class was renumbered 24xxx, with the locomotives retaining their original last three digits, except for No.D5000 which became No.24005. A total of 14 Class 24s did not survive into the TOPS era, No.D5051 being the first of the class to be withdrawn in November 1967 following a fire while working a coal train. The last Class 24 to remain in traffic was No.24081, which was finally withdrawn in October 1980, and only a mere four locomotives survive:

Number	Location	Owner
24032	North Yorkshire Moors Railway	Privately Owned
24054	East Lancashire Railway	Bury Type 2 Group
24061	North Yorkshire Moors Railway	24061 Preservation Group
24081	Gloucester Warwickshire Railway	Privately owned

Above: *During the Nene Valley Spring Diesel Gala, No.24081 is called upon to work 2E43, the 08:30 Wansford - Peterborough, on 1st March and is seen passing Sutton Cross dragging a DMU.* **Nigel Gibbs**

Part Two: BRCW 'Scottish' Sulzers

The British Rail Class 26 diesel locomotives, also known as the BRCW Type 2, were built by the Birmingham Railway Carriage & Wagon Company (BRCW) at Smethwick, 1958 -1959. Forty seven examples were built with the last members of the class being withdrawn from active service in 1993. The first batch (Nos.D5301 - D5319) were delivered new to Hornsey TMD. Following the loan of No.D5303 to the Scottish Region from 1958, a further twenty seven locomotives of a slightly modified design (D5320 - D5346) were delivered to the Scottish Region between April and October 1959. Here, all the Class remained for the duration of their working life.

The Class 26 were 'maids of all work' and could be found on a wide variety of duties; the Inverness based examples were particularly associated with the Far North Line and Kyle of Lochalsh Line. They also worked over the Highland Line on Glasgow / Edinburgh expresses, working in multiple, duties also shared with locally based Class 24s.

The Haymarket engines were latterly more associated with freight traffic, and the first seven locomotives (D5300 - D5306, later renumbered Nos. 26007, 26001 - 26006, respectively) were given slow speed control apparatus for use on MGR coal trains. The Class 26 was the forerunner of the Class 27, which was also built by BRCW during 1961 & 1962. Fortunately, a staggering thirteen Class 26 locomotives survive:

Number	Location	Number	Location
26001	Caledonian Railway	26024	Bo'Ness & Kinneil Railway
26002	Strathspey Railway	26025	Strathspey Railway
26004	Bo'Ness & Kinneil Railway	26035	Caledonian Railway
26007	Barrow Hil	26038	Cardiff Canton
26010	Bo'Ness & Kinneil Railway	26040	Methil
26011	Barrow Hill	26043	Glos. & Warwickshire Railway
26014	Caledonian Railway		

Part Three: D821 'Greyhound' & D832 'Onslaught'

The BR Western Region opted for hydraulic transmission with lightweight alloy construction for its new 'Warship' class diesel locomotives to replace steam locomotive operation; two reasons being the stiff gradients between Exeter and Plymouth on the London to Penzance route and a need to save fuel.

On 14th July 1958, a gleaming D800 stood at London's Paddington station, complete with headboard proclaiming 'First 2,200hp Diesel-Hydraulic Locomotive built in British Railways workshops - Swindon 1958'. The fleet would total 71 examples, but were scorned by many enthusiasts, as they heralded the end for the 4-6-0 King and Castle class steam locomotives of "God's Wonderful Railway."

The 'Warships' were built in three batches:

D800 - D832 : Swindon Works
D833 - D865 : North British Locomotive Company (NBL)
D866 - D870 : Swindon Works

The NBL-built 'Warships' differed mechanically; the Swindon ones used Maybach engines connected to Mekydro hydraulic transmissions, the NBL examples MAN engines and Voith transmissions. However, all 'Warships' were named after naval vessels, except No.D800 'Sir Brian Robertson' after the Chairman of the British Transport Commission at the time and No.812 'Royal Naval Reserve 1859-1959'. All those named after Royal Navy vessels also bore a subtitle "Warship Class" in smaller letters.

In 1967, due to a bias against hydraulic transmission in the higher echelons of BR, it was decreed that all the WR's diesel-hydraulics were non-standard and should be withdrawn as soon as possible. As the 'Warships' were vacuum braked and fitted with only steam heating capabilities, the end was probably inevitable, being unable to work newer designs of air-braked ETH coaching stock.

Early withdrawal meant that no 'Warship' carried a TOPS number. The first Class member to be withdrawn was No.801 'Vanguard' on 3rd August 1968 and following a period of mass withdawals in 1971, No.832 'Onslaught' became the last withdrawal on 16th December 1972. Only No.821 'Greyhound' and No.832 'Onslaught' survived the cutting torch.

Above: *It could be Wick or Thurso from a bygone era, but it is actually Bo'Ness on 3rd May and No.26024 preparing to leave with a three coach train, forming the 16:15hrs service to Birkhill.* **Jim Ramsay**

Below: *A majestic sight looking across the Firth of Forth towards Longannet power station. During the Bo'Ness & Kinneil Railway Diesel Gala held on 26th April, No.26024 is piloted by Class 27 No.27001 and is seen arriving at Bo'Ness with a timetabled service from Birkhill.* **Carl Gorse**

Above: *Pure nostalgia!*

This is the ex-Caledonian Railway, near Montrose, with No.D5314 (26014) in original green livery awaiting departure from Brechin with the 11:00hrs to Bridge of Dun on Monday, 5th May. No.27024 (ex-D5370) can be seen stabled in front of the shed and No.D5301 (26001) is at the buffer stops.

Below: *Displaying Railfreight black diamond coal sector decals, No.26004 sits in Bo'Ness Yard awaiting overhaul, one of seven examples allocated to Haymarket TMD. These locomotives were fitted with slow-speed controls for use on internal Scottish MGR duties, bringing coal to Cockenzie power station from three main sources, Bilston Glen, Blindwells and Monktonhall.* **Jim Ramsay (2)**

D821 'Greyhound'

Above: *The 'Warships' appeared in three different liveries during their working life - green, maroon and blue, in that particular order, and all three are illustrated, so you can judge for yourself which you prefer. The first image shows No.821 'Greyhound', carrying the original green livery, on display at a weekend rail Fair at Exeter Riverside on 30th April 1994.*

Below: *It may be hard to believe, but this is also No.821, photographed six weeks previously on 19th March, at Old Oak Common Open Day wearing BR Blue livery.*

D832 *'Onslaught'*

Above: *I was under the mistaken impression that turning out a locomotive in a livery not worn during its working life was more a modern day practice (eg. No.40145 in BR Blue Large logo), but it seems not. Here we see No.832 passing Burrs on the East Lancs. Railway with the 17:00hrs Bury - Rawtensall service on 8th May 1993. The locomotive has been painted in black and the paintwork looks rather 'blotchy' in appearance.* **Hugh Ballantyne (3)**

Below: *Two classic designs of Western Region diesel hydraulic locomotive combine to double-head the 13:40 Bishops Lydeard - Minehead at Woolston on the West Somerset Railway, Saturday, 16th June 2007, during a 'Mixed Traffic' Gala weekend. The locomotives are No.832 'Onslaught' and Class 52 No.D1010 'Western Campaigner', both turned out in maroon livery. Unfortunately, the day was slightly spoilt by the photographer getting soaked to the skin and losing a Blackberry!* **Chris Perkins**

WELCOME BACK SVR

2007 proved to be a very difficult year for the Severn Valley Railway (SVR), due primarily to massive storms in June and July. This caused damage to the line in a total of 45 separate locations, forcing closure between Bewdley and Bridgnorth for several months - according to the BBC, the equivalent of two weeks rain fell along the Severn Valley in the space of just thirty minutes in mid-June!

No one could have foreseen the devastation that resulted and work was immediately put in hand to repair the damage with the Railway planning to reopen fully between Kidderminster and Bridgnorth in early 2008. In June 2007, an emergency appeal was set in motion to raise funds for the repair bill, which would include £500,000 from the SVR's insurers and a grant of £750,000 from Advantage West Midlands. The initial bill was estimated at £1.25 million, but revised upwards to £2.5 million as a result of further damage following more rain and flooding in late July 2007.

The response from the general public was fantastic with calls and messages of goodwill, plus substantial donations being made towards the appeal. Fortunately, the Brignorth - Hampton Loade section eventually re-opens on 9th February; the first passenger train to Hampton Loade since 19th June 2007 departs on time at 10:30hrs and the line reopens fully on Good Friday, 21st March.

These three images are from the SVR Diesel Gala, held over three days in April, and is the first such event to be held after the flood damage repairs. The event attracts over 2,000 visitors.

Above: *'Western' Class 52 No.D1013 'Western Ranger' accelerates away from Sandbourne Viaduct hauling the 10:27 Bridgnorth - Kidderminster, on a day when it would have been nice to have seen the sun shine!*

Top Right: *This particular Gala is christened 'Slugfest' due to the eagerly awaited pairing of Mirrlees-engined Class 37/9 locomotives No.37901 'Mirrlees Pioneer' + No. 37906; enthusiasts are not disappointed, as we can see in this view of the two 'Slugs' passing Seven Hills with the 11:03 Kidderminster - Bewdley service.*

Bottom Right: *Class 20s running singularly, let alone nose end first, has never been common practice on the main line, but does take place during the gala, as this this delightful scene shows. No.D8188 (20188) exits Bewdley Tunnel hauling the 11:46 Kidderminster - Arley, a locomotive which gained fame in the 1995 Bond film 'Goldeneye', when it featured as an escape train, with the addition of armour plating to give the impression of a Russian armoured locomotive. All three images were taken on 25th April.* **Richard Jones (3)**

A DAY on the CLAY

Above: *The Bodmin & Wenford Railway runs for 3.5 miles from Bodmin's Parkway and General stations, plus 3.0 miles from Bodmin General to Boscarne Junction. On 15th March, a special photographic charter is organised featuring Class 37/0 No.37142 on a demonstration china clay freight service and this is seen in a beautifully wooded section of the line at Charlie's Gate.*

Below: *Later in the day, No.37142 is seen again passing Charlie's Bridge alongside the A38 during a downpour. The 'Growler' was purchased by the Bodmin & Wenford Mainline Diesel Group in May 2003 and was started up in June 2004 for the first time in preservation.* **Robert Sherwood (2)**

THE 'PULLMAN' RETURNS

Below: *Having received two superb images of No.73101 'The Royal Alex' working the Llangollen diesel gala and not being able to decide which to use, I opted for both - hope you don't mind! On 12th April, the 'ED' pauses at picturesque Berwyn on the 14:35 Llangollen - Carrog, with the rambling spring melt waters of the River Doo below and to the left of the train. The locomotive. had a stint at the SVR in 2007 to help with reconstruction work following the storm damage, in return for which the SVR gave it a fresh coat of its unique Pullman livery.* **Mark Riley**

Bottom: *On the previous day, the celebrity 'ED' looks splendid hauling a 5-coach rake of near-matching chocolate & cream coaches on the curve approaching Pentrefelyn, while working the 15:15 Carrog - Llangollen.* **Fred Kerr**

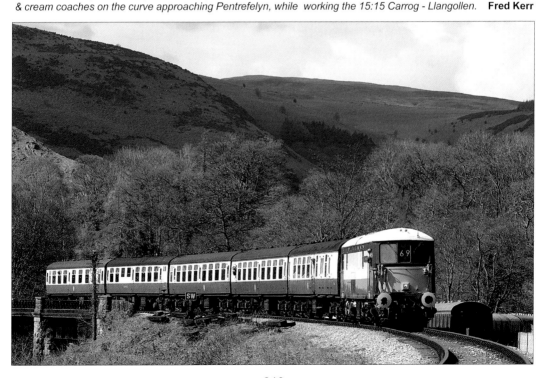

OFF THE PEG

Above: *Apart from the obvious attraction of classic traction, Heritage Lines also provide the railway historian with excellent examples of semaphore signalling and a small selection are included here. In this view at Bo'Ness on the Bo'Ness & Kinneil Railway, Class 37/0 No.37175 passes an upper quadrant three-way junction signal, for routes of three different speeds or importance.*
Carl Gorse

Above: *This is a fine signal gantry, which houses an assortment of semaphores; eight controlling the running lines and sidings at Bury Bolton Street on the East Lancashire Railway. 'Deltic' No.55022 'Royal Scots Grey' arrives at the station on a dreary 15th March, working a Rawtenstall - Heywood service.* **Mark Riley**

Below: *This is another example of a three-way junction signal, but this time of GWR lower quadrant design at Totnes on the South Devon Railway. You will notice that the central post houses a 'subsidiary signal' (ie.small red arm with horizontal white stripe) mounted below the stop arm, in order to give a driver special information about the section ahead. For example, when off, a letter C, S or W will be displayed, thus:*

C: Calling-on signal. The section ahead is occupied.

S: Shunt-ahead signal. This indicates that the signal may be passed only for shunting purposes.

W: Warning signal. This indicates Section Clear but Station or Junction Blocked.

This image depicts Class 20s, No.20110 in BR Blue + No.20118 in Railfreight Grey with red sole bar, double heading the 14:02 Totnes - Buckfastleigh service during a South Devon Railway Diesel Gala. **Robert Sherwood**

SWANAGE
A Diesel Gala To Remember

During Spring 2008, there is a veritable feast of diesel galas being organised on heritage lines across the country but, perhaps, one stands out above them all - Swanage!

The selection of diesels on offer during the three-day gala being held between 9th - 11th May is tremendous, with an incredible six main line locomotives making the journey south for the event:

Nos. 20096 / 37275 / 37906 / D444 *'Exeter'* / 66724 *'Drax Power Station'* / 73107 *'Spitfire'*

In addition, Knights Rail Services Class 07 shunting locomotive and 4-VEP EMU No. 3417 *'Gordon Pettitt'* join the fray - Harry Needle Railway Company decide to send their locomotive (No.20096) adorned with metals sub-sector decals and Thornaby TMD Kingfisher emblems.

Images:

Above: *With Corfe Castle dominating the high ground in the background, Class 37/9 No.37906 explodes into action hauling a rake of ex-Southern Region coaches plus Class 33/0 No.D6515 (33012) in tow.*

Page 218:

Top Left: *Looking down from the elevated vantage point of Corfe Castle, Class 66/7 No.66724 'Drax Power Station' departs from the station heading for Norden with Class 73/1 No.73107 DIT on the rear; another special train involving Class 50 No.D444 (50044) can be seen in the distance.*

Bottom Left: *The vicinity around Corfe Castle abounds in good vantage points to photograph train services, such as Corfe Common, where an immaculate Class 37/0 No.37275 is seen passing with BRCW No.D6515 DIT on the rear of the train.*

Page 219:

Top Right: *Double-heading at diesel galas is very popular and can provide some interesting combinations, such as Class 20 No.20096 piloting No.37906 through Corfe Common.*

Bottom Right: *Meanwhile, looking in the opposite direction during the first day of the gala, No.73107 + No.20096 double-head the 4-VEP through Corfe Common.* **Carl Gorse (5)**

Opposite: *What a colourful convoy - following the Swanage three-day gala, No.66724 tows Nos.20096, 37275, 37906 and D444 through Basingstoke on 12th May, running as 0Z74, Furzebrook - Kidderminster.* **Nic Joynson**

KEIGHLEY

&

WORTH

40th Anniversary

The Keighley & Worth Valley Railway (KWVR) celebrates its 40th anniversary in 2008 following the re-opening of the line in 1968 by holding a diesel gala on 7th June to commemorate the event. It is a standard gauge branch line, joining the national railway network at Keighley, West Yorkshire, and runs 5-miles up the Worth Valley to Oxenhope. Other stations on the Line include Oakworth (location of the film 'The Railway Children') and Haworth (former home of the Brontë family).

The Line was built in 1867 by local mill owners and eventually became part of the London, Midland & Scottish Railway in 1924 and British Railways (BR) in 1948. BR closed the branch in 1962 but, as a result of public pressure, a preservation society was formed which created a Company to buy the Line outright, lease access into Keighley station and operate a regular public service. Initially, diesel railcars were purchased to operate a daily passenger service, a diesel locomotive to work goods trains and several steam locomotives and carriages. The end result is superb - congratulations KWVR!

Above: *DRS Class 37/0 No.37087 is named 'Keighley & Worth Valley Railway' to commemorate the 40th Anniversary and is seen running round at Oxenhope before working the 15:00 Oxenhope - Keighley; Class mate No.D6737 (37037) is already on the train, while Class 52 No.D1023 'Western Fusilier' awaits her turn. To complement KWVR's small fleet of diesels (Nos.20031 and 25059), visiting locos, Nos.20087, 20110, D7612, 31108, D6737, 37087, plus D1023 from the National Railway Museum, all participate at the Gala.* **Ralf Edge**

Top: *Nameplate of No.37087.* **Carl Gorse**

Above: *An interesting combination .... green-liveried Class 37/0 No.D6737 (37037) + Railfreight-Grey Class 31/1 No.31108 double-head a Oxenhope - Keighley service approaching Damems passing loop.* **Carl Gorse**

Below: *Oops! Visiting WCRC Class 47/7 No.47760 derails at Oxenhope, which is very unfortunate, as it occurs on the occasion of the KWVR's 40th Anniversary celebrations, preventing intended main line steam specials taking place. It also has a siginificant impact on the Worth Valley's own services. At the scene, there seems to be an air of apathy as a throng of official looking bystanders await a remedial course of action!* **Neil Harvey**

ACKNOWLEDGEMENTS

Contributors:

My sincere thanks go to all the people named below, who have kindly contributed images for inclusion in this title, without which this book would not be possible. I have also provided details of respective website addresses, should you wish to see more of these contributors fine work.

BALL, Ian	Thirsk	northeastheavy.fototopic.net
BALLANTYNE, Hugh	Eccleshall	
BINCH, John	Harborne	
BUCKLEY, Justin	Erdington	ticketmans.fototopic.net
CAMERON, Donald	Milngavie	
DOIG, Jamie	London	
EDGE, Ralf	Leicester	ralfedge.co.uk
GATEHOUSE, Don	Bromsgrove	
GIBBS, Nigel	Bedford	
GORSE, Carl	Hartlepool	37682.fototopic.net
HARVEY, Neil	Halifax	neilharvey4789.fototopic.net
HAZELDEN, Alan	Tunbridge Wells	
HEMMING, Mike	Wellington	
HOUSTON, Guy	Larbert	guyhouston.fototopic.net
JONES, Richard	Chislehurst	railphotos.demeseo.com
JOYNSON, Nic	Ringwood	
KERR, Fred	Southport	
McGOVERN, Keith	Mussleburgh	
MORRIS, Geoff	Chester	
NAYLOR, Andrew	Carnforth	andrewstransport.fototopic.net
PERKINS, Chris	Weston-super-Mare	chrisperkins.fpic.co.uk
PLUMB, Geoff	Aylesbury	geoff-plumb.fototopic.net
RAMSAY, Jim	Carnoustie	tayrail.fototopic.net
RILEY, Mark	Wrexham	mark-riley.fototopic.net
RUDD, John	Peterborough	
SCOTCHMAN, Iain	Shenfield	
SHERWOOD, Robert	Paignton	southwestrailways.fototopic.net
SLOCOMBE, Nick	London	trainsofthewesternworld.fototopic.net
SMALL, Andy	Leicester	andy4585.fototopic.net
SPRAY, Richard	Mold	
STRACEY, Dave	Chinnor	
TANDY, Peter	Stratford on Avon	petertandy.co.uk
TINDALL, Mick	Sutton in Ashfield	mpt-trains.fototopic.net
WELHAM, James	Great Leighs	jameswelham.fototopic.net
WRIGHT, Michael	Chessington	37517slocopics.fotoblog.co.uk

Previously:

Page 222: *One of the intrepid members of the East Midlands Railway Photographic Society captured this excellent image during a photographic charter held on the Froxfield Railway using Class 20/0 No.20154, visiting from the Great Central Railway on 13th July. The locomotive appears in post-1973 numbers, full yellow ends and weathered in BR green livery, seen here heading a short rake of vacuum braked mineral wagons at Froxfield Colliery; a scene very reminiscent of a colliery branch line in the 1970's - nostalgia indeed!*   **Ralf Edge**

Page 223: *Completely overhauled and looking superb!*

This is Class 37/5 No.37518, finished in Railfreight-grey livery with red stripe and sporting a Thornaby TMD Kingfisher emblem, which the locomotive carried in the 1980s. Here, the 'tractor' passes over a very calm River Nene on the approach to Wansford Station on the Nene Valley Railway, working a a 'Driver Experience' special service from Peterborough NVR.   **James Welham**